Tough Parenting
FOR
Dangerous Times

Tough Parenting
FOR
Dangerous Times

ANDY BUSTANOBY

with *VERNE BECKER*

ZondervanPublishingHouse
Grand Rapids, Michigan
A Division of HarperCollinsPublishers

Tough Parenting for Dangerous Times
Copyright © 1992 by André Bustanoby

Requests for information should be addressed to:
Zondervan Publishing House
Grand Rapids, Michigan 49530

Library of Congress Cataloging-in-Publication Data

Bustanoby, André.
  Tough parenting for dangerous times / André Bustanoby with Verne
Becker
    p. cm.
  Includes bibliographical references.
  ISBN 0-310-54901-9 (paper)
    1. Child rearing—United States. 2. Parenting—United States.
I. Becker, Verne. II. Title.
HQ769.B84 1992
649'.1—dc20   91–40353
                                                         CIP

All Scripture quotations, unless otherwise noted, are taken from the HOLY
BIBLE: NEW INTERNATIONAL VERSION® (North American Edition).
Copyright © 1973, 1978, 1984, by the International Bible Society. Used by
permission of Zondervan Publishing House.

"NIV" and "New International Version" are registered in the United States
Patent and Trademark Office by the International Bible Society.

Edited by Linda Vanderzalm
Interior designed by Kim Koning
Cover designed by Terry Dugan Design

Printed in the United States of America

92 93 94 95 96 97 / AM / 10 9 8 7 6 5 4 3 2 1

Contents

	Introduction	7
1.	Understanding Our Children's Development	17
2.	When Self-Centeredness Is Okay: Birth to Age One	26
3.	Helping Your Baby Become Self-Confident: Age One	43
4.	Taming the Terrible Twos: Age Two	63
5.	Just When We Think the Storm Is Over: Ages Three and Four	83
6.	Capitalizing on Cooperation: Age Five	104
7.	The Mystery Years—What Is This Child Thinking? Ages Six Through Ten	118
8.	Good-bye Childhood: Ages Eleven and Twelve	150
9.	Helping Them Become Adolescents: Age Thirteen	167
10.	Helping Them Become Adults: Ages Fourteen Through Seventeen	184
11.	Leaving Home: Age Eighteen to Young Adulthood	206
12.	When Things Get Out of Hand	222
13.	You Can Do It	238
	Resources	247
	Notes	251

Introduction

I had spent a very emotionally draining day counseling troubled families. I was especially concerned about Tena, a fourteen-year-old girl who had attempted suicide. Perhaps this had made me emotionally vulnerable to what I saw on television that night as I sat down to relax and unwind.

I flipped to the movie channel and found *Heartburn*, starring Meryl Streep and Jack Nicholson. Streep played the part of a verbally battered wife and mother, and Nicholson played the part of a hateful, abusive husband and father. They had a darling five-year-old girl.

Throughout the movie the father verbally battered both the mother and daughter with unbearable meanness. And the two females took the abuse. But something in the final scene moved me deeply.

While the three of them ate dinner amidst the verbal barrage, a grim determination grew on the mother's face. Something had changed. In the middle of her husband's verbal lashing, she firmly said, "That's enough." She got up from the table, took her daughter by the hand, and went to the bedroom. There, she got her suitcases and began to pack their clothes. The father followed, berating them, telling her they would be back, that they would never make it without him.

The scene then cut to the airport. As the mother and daughter walked to the plane, the haunting strains of a child's song began in the background, playing in a four-part round. They boarded the plane and took their seat, with the daughter straddled on mother's lap, facing her. The mother hugged her and then began to sing the song:

The itsy-bitsy spider climbed up the waterspout;
Down came the rain and washed the spider out.
Out came the sun and dried up all the rain;
And the itsy-bitsy spider climbed up the spout again.

As the mother sang it again, her daughter joined in.

I couldn't control my tears. As I watched the plane taxi to the runway, a great chorus of voices joined in the song. I started to sob uncontrollably, thinking, "That little girl is going to survive. Her mother has taught her well that itsy-bitsy spiders may have bad things happen to them; life can be a washout. But you don't give up. When the rain is over, you climb up the spout again. Every time circumstances overwhelm you, you come back. And you keep doing it."

Then I cried for Tena. This was a lesson she had never learned. Her parents never permitted her to face the pressures of life. When she was little, she was so protected she never developed the psychological muscles that come from climbing that spout again and again. Now, as a teenager, she had come to the place where she had to start facing the world on her own—a world that was dealing out cruelties she simply couldn't understand or handle. In her way of thinking, something was wrong. Either something was wrong with her for not being able to cope or something was wrong with other people for expecting her to put up with the bumps and bruises, which she didn't know were a normal part of life.

Tena's parents didn't understand tough parenting. They didn't realize that shielding Tena from all adversity left her undeveloped and unequipped to face it herself. They didn't understand that if Tena was going to have the character strength needed to face the rigors of life, she had to face it herself. They couldn't do it for her.

Yes, her parents were responsible to shield her from adversity that was beyond her ability to handle. But they didn't understand that one of the tough things about tough parenting is standing on the sidelines, encouraging our children while they struggle by themselves.

But how does this develop strength of character? Where does it come from? *It develops naturally—if we'll let it.*

Nature forces us to cope from the moment we are born. Indeed, the stress of being born places on us the greatest demand to cope that we'll ever experience. Imagine, for a moment, what terrible pressure we were subject to when we were pushed through that small birth canal and thrust out into a hostile environment of heat, cold, noise, and bright lights. We had to cope in order to live!

It's true that a baby's coping skills are reflexive and not a matter of choice. But the fact remains, our survival depends on our accepting nature's demands to take new steps in growth and development—demands that sometimes seem overwhelming but are always within our ability to handle.

Tough parenting means that parents understand nature's demands on children as they grow. It's called *the developmental task.* Though professional literature uses this phrase to refer to the child's task, I include parents in the task too. Parents have a responsibility to assist children in their development. We assist by permitting our children to do the hard work that only they can do yet vigilantly protecting them against pressure that is beyond their ability to handle.

Developing character strength and coping abilities is much like developing muscles through weight training. We must endure the strain and pain, keeping a positive attitude toward the grueling process, because we know the end result will be positive.

In a weight-training program, barbells aren't a cruel burden. They're the means of muscle development. In character development adversity isn't a cruel burden. It's the means of character development.

The ability to resist temptation and courageously face the demands of life begins with acceptance of adversity as the *means* of learning to cope. In life, as in sports, the saying is true: no pain, no gain.

We parents are coaches in the development of character strength. Our children will not develop that strength if we don't let them pick up the weight of life's burdens.

Certainly we have a responsibility to know how much our children can handle, to identify age-appropriate growth experiences, and to guide our children through them. But we should not try to shield them from all of life's trials. This is what tough parenting is about.

In recent years, studies of suicidal children have revealed a common thread: These children feel hapless, helpless, and hopeless. They first of all feel like victims, as if a cruel fate they don't understand has chosen to club them with an emotional blow that they don't deserve. These hapless victims, who never learned to accept adversity as a friend, feel helpless to do anything about it. They're at a loss to understand why they are going through this terrible experience, and they don't know what to do about it. As this hapless, helpless feeling wears them down, they finally feel hopeless.

Over the past thirty years the suicide rate among young men and women ages fifteen to twenty-four has risen approximately 250 percent. The United States now ranks the highest in the world, passing Japan and Sweden, countries long troubled with youth suicide.

If researchers are correct, the problem of youth suicide

is going to get worse. According to one source, by the year 2005, the youth-suicide rate will increase as much as 144 percent for males ages ten to fourteen. For males ages twenty to twenty-four, it will increase 146 percent. The rate of increase among young women may be as high as 120 percent.[1]

These are, indeed, dangerous times for our children. Many children are ill-prepared to face the rigors of life. But they are ill-prepared in part because many parents don't understand the art of tough parenting. The very fact that you are now reading this book about tough parenting gives your children a better chance for survival.

We shouldn't think, however, that tough parenting produces kids who are unfeeling or insensitive. They feel the pain of adversity and understand the pain that others feel. Tough parenting teaches children that trials are a normal part of life. Tough parenting lets children feel the weight of difficulties and accept the responsibility for carrying it. Our children develop character strength not *in spite of* adversity but *because of* it.

Tough parenting understands this concept and the importance of having an accepting attitude toward the burdens we must carry. Our children catch our attitudes. If we react to unexpected problems with acceptance and a positive attitude that looks for growth through coping, then our kids most likely will adopt the same attitude. Though we hurt, we don't ask, Why me? If trials are part of the maturing process, then the appropriate question is, Why *not* me?

Because learning to cope with life's hurts is so important to the maturing process, tough parenting means that we lovingly but firmly teach kids to tackle and solve their own problems and accept pain as a normal part of growing up. For toddlers, it may mean letting them pick themselves up after they've fallen. For teenagers who insist on wearing fashionable clothes with a high price tag, it may mean telling them to get a job and pay for what they want, accept a cheaper item, or do without. We should expect teenagers to want what the other kids want, but they need to be ready to pay the price for their wants.

Doing for our children what they ought to be doing for themselves, more than anything else, hinders maturity and is the biggest single reason why American children are unable to cope with the dangerous times in which they live. They grow up with unrealistic expectations and as a result are unable to handle disappointment.

Tough parenting must go hand-in-hand with intelligent parenting that understands the various stages of development our kids go through. We must know what developmental tasks we are to encourage in our children at each stage. What should they be expected to do? How can we encourage our children to do what they need to do? What problems must they be expected to overcome? How much parental protectiveness is too much?

For example, the major developmental task one-year-olds face is achieving self-confidence. This means that parents let them try new tasks and encourage their success. To do this, we may have to put up with a messy house or disrupted schedule. Tough parenting isn't only tough on the kids; it's tough on parents too. It means that we need to be willing to sacrifice some of our comfort to do the all-important job of raising kids who can face a dangerous world. A messy house or disrupted schedule isn't nearly as important as giving our children the opportunity to develop as nature intends.

How tough we are as parents will be influenced largely by the memories of our own childhood. As children, were we so overwhelmed by disappointment that we are determined that *our* children will not experience what we experienced? Certainly we ought to protect our children from overwhelming heartaches or any weight too great for their stage of development. We don't want to expose them to life-threatening situations. But we do teach them that physical and emotional bumps and bruises are a normal part of life, essential to building coping skills.

Some parents find it hard to teach their children how to cope with difficult times because they themselves have poor patterns of coping with difficulty. Perhaps they deny that difficulties exist, or they minimize them. What they suppose is a spiritual outlook on life really is a Pollyanna approach that is ill-suited to the task of tough parenting.

On the other hand, we may have enjoyed a trouble-free childhood and now feel that our children should have a trouble-free childhood too. But it may be that we don't remember the bumps and bruises we experienced because they actually were wholesome growth experiences.

Children feel lots of hurts, but part of learning to deal successfully with those hurts is *their* willingness to accept those hurts and *our* willingness as parents to expect this of them. We must not rob our children of healthy emotional development by being overly protective.

We must be careful, however, that we don't deliberately make life tough for our kids, thinking that it helps them learn to cope. Life naturally deals every child enough hardship.

Parents familiar with Dr. Thomas Gordon's book *Parent Effectiveness Training* (Peter H. Wyden, Inc., 1970) will find *Tough Parenting for Dangerous Times* an important addition to the art of parenting. I heartily agree with Gordon's no-lose approach to parenting. Most children are cooperative and are willing to negotiate differences with their parents. We should negotiate differences as much as possible.

Tough Parenting goes a step further and answers two questions that parents often ask: What happens when children thwart all parental attempts to negotiate differences? and What happens when children challenge the limits put on them and want to negotiate the nonnegotiable?

To break the deadlock, parents sometimes need to be "authoritative." When it's done with a caring consistency, our children will be far more cooperative than we ever imagined. Sometimes they just want to know how far they can push us.

Authoritative parents differ from *authoritarian* parents in that authoritative parents are more thoughtful and sympathetic. The wants and needs of their children are important. But they do recognize that parents have a God-given mandate to control their children. Sometimes a parent must say to the child, "I understand what you want, but I'm sorry, I can't do it." But it's done lovingly, consistently, and only when boundaries or limits are in question.

Our task isn't to make life tougher for our kids but to provide a loving, caring environment in which our children are permitted to face demands they can handle. It's an environment in which our children learn that it isn't a cruel fate that dishes out hardship, but a loving God who uses trials to help us grow, a loving God who is constantly at hand to give us wisdom necessary to cope.

Understanding Toughmindedness

The dictionary defines *toughmindedness* as "shrewd and unsentimental, practical, realistic." Toughminded parents are those who approach their parenting responsibility practically and realistically, without getting hooked by sentimentality.

But while toughmindedness is a psychological concept, I firmly believe it is also a spiritual concept. Since all truth is

God's truth, psychology and theology should agree. And they do. The Bible says, "Consider it pure joy, my brothers, whenever you face trials of many kinds, because you know that the testing of your faith develops perseverance. Perseverance must finish its work so that you may be *mature and complete*, not lacking anything" (James 1:2–4, emphasis added). I like the Living Bible's paraphrase of this passage: "When the way is rough, your patience has a chance to grow. So let it grow, and don't try to squirm out of your problems. For when your patience is finally in full bloom, then you will be ready for anything, strong in character, full and complete."

Spiritual toughmindedness requires us to understand three things.

First, trials, which can be anything from adversity to temptation to sin, are permitted to assist us in achieving emotional and spiritual maturity. Because of this, James urges us not only to accept trials, but also to consider it *pure joy* when we face them. We need to know that God isn't trying to hurt or hinder us. As a loving Father he wants us to develop into mature people. God's permitting trial is a *loving* act.

Second, the method God uses is the testing of our faith. This simply means that trials force us to ask ourselves if we believe that God is truly *God*. Is he the all-wise Father who loves us and is determined to bring us to maturity by means that are beyond our understanding? James uses Job as an example of this process. He says, "You have heard of Job's perseverance and have seen what the Lord finally brought about" (James 5:11). Job went through adversity that tested his ability to trust God even though Job didn't understand what God was doing. Forced to endure trial that he didn't understand, Job took a giant step of spiritual growth.

Trial is to character development what weights are to muscle building. If we want to develop our physique through weight training, then we must force our muscles to endure the weights in various kinds of exercises and through many repetitions. A good weight-training coach knows how much weight we can bear and how many repetitions in each exercise will produce optimum muscle development. Just as repeated endurance of the weights produces muscles, repeated endurance of trial produces character. The apostle Paul agrees when he says, "We also rejoice in our sufferings, because we know that suffering produces perseverance; perseverance, character . . ." (Rom. 5:3–4).

Third, trial is designed to produce not merely a passive acceptance but an active faith. James tells us that if we fall short in wisdom, we ought to ask God for it. What does he mean by this?

It's one thing to be at peace because we're confident that God knows what he's doing. But what are we to do as events unfold? Enduring trial isn't a passive act. In weight training, we have to do something with the weight. Similarly, when we face difficulty, we need to do something about the trial. We are to ask the coach how to handle the weight. We are to say, "God, I believe you know what you're doing. I'm excited about the prospect of being a better, more mature person as a result of this. But what do you want me to do with this weight? Show me how to handle it so that it will optimize my growth."

Tough parenting allows our children to *face* difficulties, not squirm out of them. Tough parenting knows that by facing rough times and by developing coping skills, our children will be ready for anything, strong in character, full and complete.

1

Understanding
Our Children's Development

In order to be tough parents, we must understand child development and the predictable stages that our children go through in their growth. We need to understand the kind of guidance and patience our children need at each developmental stage, when we should let our children face adversity by themselves, and how much and what kind of adversity is beyond our children's ability to cope with at each developmental stage—in short, when to intervene.

Of Kids and Crabs

Our children are much like the Chesapeake Bay blue crab. I'm not talking about the blue crab's feisty reputation, though kids can be crabby creatures. The comparison I have in mind is the blue crab's developmental process.

The blue crab comes into the world developing a shell quickly to protect it from predators. As long as it has a hard shell, the crab lives quite comfortably with the rest of the marine life in the Bay.

But frequently throughout its life, the blue crab becomes unsociable and goes into hiding. The reason is that it's going to lose its protective shell. It's going to molt.

Losing the protective shell is part of the growth process. It can't grow in size, strength, or ability to reproduce as long as it's confined by its protective shell. So it molts.

Once the hard shell is gone, the tender membrane underneath can grow and add the more adult features the crab needs in order to be fully developed. But molting is a difficult time for the crab.

During the time that the crab is in molt, known as "instar," it hides because it's vulnerable to predators. But once the new growth has taken place, a new and larger shell forms to accommodate the new growth. The blue crab is then ready to come out of hiding and return to its normal sociable behavior.

This molting process takes place from eighteen to twenty-three times in a crab's lifetime.

Human beings go through a similar experience. They don't have hard shells, but they have coping skills that make them feel safe and help them to be at peace with themselves and others.

When they are ready for a new stage of growth, they experience what psychologists call *disequilibrium*. As the name suggests, it's a stage in which nothing feels right to them. Their old coping skills are no longer sufficient, but they haven't yet mastered their new coping skills. Like the blue crab shell, the old coping skills no longer fit. The old skills must be shed in order for new skills—for the next stage of growth—to develop. And once they do, the child returns to a more confident and sociable way of life called *equilibrium*. Like the crab with a new shell, children again feel safe with their newly developed coping skills.

Parents sometimes feel that something is wrong when their children are in disequilibrium, going through a molt. But nothing's wrong. They really *are*, as we say, "going through a stage."

We must be careful at these stages of disequilibrium. If we protect our children too much, we will keep them from the demands of further growth and all the frustrations and insecurities that go with it. Instead, as James writes, "Consider it pure joy" when our children take another step of growth. Wouldn't it be sad if they remained small and undeveloped?

No one likes to see helpless five-month-old babies cry because they are frustrated at their attempts to crawl. It tugs at our hearts to hear them scream because their mommy has left the room. But we understand and permit their unhappiness. They're going through a psychological molt. We encourage them to keep trying, and we reinforce their successes. We show them that when their mommy leaves, she comes back. But we can't do for them what they must do for themselves. With our encouragement, they must do this hard work by themselves.

Parents can be sure that children, like crabs, do return to equilibrium when they've completed a new stage of growth. Our children will again feel secure and able to cope with their environment if we give them time, patience, and encouragement. But remember, *we can't do it for them*. And we must convey the attitude that these upsetting stages of disequilibrium are a normal part of growing up.

Our children's developmental and coping skills will come naturally as long as we don't interfere with the process, don't relieve them of the struggle, or try to do it for them. I recently talked to a new mother who was awed by the process. She asked me cautiously, "How many times will our children go through a psychological molt?"

When I told her, "About as many times as a crab does," she just looked down and shook her head in despair.

Another similarity between children and blue crabs is the rate of change. In the very young crab, the period between molts lasts only ten to fifteen days. As the crab grows older, it molts less frequently, going anywhere from thirty to fifty days between molts. By the time it's an adult, its molting is just about complete.

In children, changes occur most rapidly early in their lives. As they grow older, that rate of molt slows down. We'll see that children from birth to their first birthday go through equilibrium, disequilibrium, and back to equilibrium about five times. After age two, a time of disequilibrium, they go through the stages of equilibrium and disequilibrium every other year.

Psychologists cluster these yearly developmental periods into larger groups of several years and give them names (infancy, preschool, adolescence, etc.). These periods are roughly ages birth through five, six through ten, eleven through twelve, thirteen, fourteen through seventeen, and eighteen to young adulthood. Because no uniform names have been given to these periods, I'll just call them milestones and identify them by age (see chart on pages 23–25).

Stages of equilibrium and disequilibrium, occurring approximately at yearly intervals (with the exception of ages eight and nine), mark the gradual stages of development and the immediate developmental tasks. The milestones mark major steps in the long-term developmental task.

For example, age five is a milestone. Children no longer struggle with reconciling their needs and the needs of others. They have more growing to do when faced with conflicting needs, but they find that their needs and the needs of others aren't irreconcilable.

They must go through bouts of self-centeredness twice (at ages two and four) before they conquer it and come to a milestone of cooperation. The major equilibrium they experience at ages five, ten, and sixteen roughly coincides with arrival at these milestones.

The ages that these developments occur, whether they be yearly stages or milestones, *are only approximate*. Some children arrive earlier and some later than others. So avoid comparing your children unfavorably with others if they're slow in arriving at their yearly developmental stages and multi-year milestones.

If your infant's development seems to be slow, consult your doctor. Remember that development involves the whole person. For example, what may seem to be slow cognitive development (perception, memory, and judgment) may be a physical problem—the result of seeing or hearing problems. Lack of motor development may be a physical rather than a mental deficiency.

We also should be careful not to compare our children unfavorably with others when our children are exceptionally difficult. One mother told me, "My child is *never* in equilibrium. Life is always a turmoil with him." Some children temperamentally are more difficult than others. If that's the case with your child, your only comparison of developmental stages may be "difficult" and "more difficult." You should, however, be able to see progress in their cognitive, physical/emotional, and social development. Be very positive about their development and reinforce their positive feelings about it.

The chart "Age, Stage, and Milestone" offers a picture of the developmental process. The chart is an attempt to simplify understanding of the developmental process, but it runs the risk of oversimplification. Though I show the developmental tasks taking place during the stages of disequilibrium, it doesn't mean that nothing happens during the stages of equilibrium. Equilibrium is the time to consolidate lessons learned. And equilibrium and disequilibrium do not occur at precise yearly intervals. These are only approximations, with change occurring gradually over many months. In fact, change often occurs so gradually that we are unaware the child is moving toward disequilibrium until there's a blowup or crisis.

Rather than lose parents in a lot of detail, I stress the most important features of child development: equilibrium and disequilibrium, with the emphasis on disequilibrium. I stress disequilibrium because parents tend to think that something's wrong with their children when it happens. Let's look at it positively and facilitate it. Don't try to ignore it or make it go away.

When your child starts disequilibrium, something good—new growth—is happening. And it can't occur until the child sheds the protective shell of earlier growth. Though this is a troublesome time for both children and parents, we should welcome it as an advance toward maturity. Parents who understand this will be less inclined to handle the experience negatively and will look for opportunities to facilitate growth.

Our children's development from birth to adulthood is a jarring process. We'll like the equilibrium and dislike the disequilibrium. But just like the feisty blue crab, our children must have their times of molt and disorganization if they're to grow and be ready for the next developmental stage.

CHART 1

AGE	STAGE	MILESTONE
	Equilibrium or disequilibrium; immediate developmental task	Long-term developmental task
Birth to Age 1	Children go through five periods of equilibrium (4, 16, 28, 40, 52 weeks) and disequilibrium in the intervening weeks. *Developmental task:* bonding with their mother.	
Age 1	Equilibrium moves toward disequilibrium as children attempt to move about and understand their new and larger world. *Developmental task:* achieving self-confidence.	
Age 2	Equilibrium breaks down at 2½ with conflict over self-centeredness. *Developmental task:* accepting the denial of their wishes at times.	
Age 3	Equilibrium. Begin to take pleasure in pleasing others. *Developmental task:* consolidation of what they learned at age 2.	By age 5, children who began as totally self-centered people, care about the needs and feelings of others and become cooperative and are ready to learn. They have discovered that the way *they* think things should be isn't necessarily right and are willing to listen to parents and teachers.
Age 4	Disequilibrium. More adept at getting their way and return to battle of the wills. *Developmental task:* cooperating with others.	
Age 5	Equilibrium. More cooperative. Realize that their needs and other's needs aren't irreconcilable. *Developmental task:* Consolidation of what they learned at age 4.	
Age 6	Disequilibrium. Boundless energy makes sitting still difficult. New awareness of their world doesn't match their ability to understand. *Developmental task:* understanding their world.	From age 6 to 10, children discover their uniqueness and where they fit in the world, though family still is important. Equilibrium at age 10 gives a reprieve for the tough year ahead!
Age 7	Equilibrium. Inward, thoughtful, solving mysteries of life. *Developmental task:* consolidation of what they learned at age 6.	
Age 8	Disequilibrium. Speedy, exaggerates, and dramatizes. Similar to age 2. Self-confident and unaware they're a problem. *Developmental task:* cultivating peer relations with the same sex.	
Age 9	Disequilibrium. Sometimes called neurotic because of many complaints. Self-motivated. Open	

to learn. *Developmental task*: handling complaints and worries more effectively.

Age 10   Equilibrium. Generally agreeable and tolerant, but gets angry at younger siblings. *Developmental task*: consolidate the lessons learned at ages 8 and 9.

Age 11   Disequilibrium. Children caught in bind between demands of parents and peers. *Developmental task*: growing away from parents without alienating them and relating to peers without letting them be a destructive influence.

Ages 11 and 12 are a transition from childhood. Children need distance from family. Rough time for all.

Age 12   Equilibrium. Still working at breaking away from family, but they are less abrasive. Tolerance, enthusiasm, and humor make them more mellow, except toward younger siblings, who irritate them. *Development task*: consolidate the lessons learned at age 11.

Age 13   Disequilibrium. Inward, more moody than 12. *Developmental task*: New awareness of self and world opens opportunity to learn to become teenagers. Physical development raises concern over appearance. Sexual urges raise concerns about acceptance by opposite sex. Think they're learning to become adults when they're really learning to become teenagers.

Age 13 is a transition into adolescence.

Age 14   Equilibrium. Beginning to feel acceptance and to adjust to new body and sexual urges. More tolerant and social with family. *Developmental task*: consolidate the lessons learned at age 13.

Ages 14 through 17 are a time to develop independence. But quest for independence makes teenagers deny dependence on parents. Accepting dependency needs is helped by parents who assure them that they too are working toward their independence.

Age 15   Disequilibrium. New awareness of demands of adulthood are scary, yet instincts are pushing for independence. *Developmental task*: accepting dependency without fearing loss of independence.

Age 16   Equilibrium. A more adult appearance, the right to drive and work outside the home for pay give a feeling of making it as adults. Major period of consolidation. *Developmental task*: consolidate the lessons learned at age 15.

Age 17   Disequilibrium. Emotions intensify along with heterosexual interests. Denial of emotional dependency on parents often leads to conflict with or permissiveness by parents. *Developmental task*: becoming less self-centered.

Age 18 to Young Adulthood

Equilibrium. The task of becoming less self-centered is now paying off. Emerging young adults now are beginning to accept society's rules, don't feel as strongly that parents are adversaries, prepare to give up dependency on parents, and begin to become givers rather than takers. *Developmental task*: consolidating the lessons learned at age 17, which makes them less self-centered.

2

When Self-Centeredness Is Okay: Birth to Age One

"You certainly aren't going to talk about tough parenting for *babies* are you?" asked Alice, a young mother with a six-week-old infant. We had been talking about parental responsibilities and the need for tough parenting. I told her that I was working on a book about it. But the idea that such a tiny, helpless person as a baby needed tough parenting boggled her mind. "I suppose you're going to start a boot camp for babies," she teased.

Alice showed good sense as a mother. She understood that her newborn daughter, Kim, was a bundle of undeveloped instincts reaching out reflexively. She understood that Kim wasn't fussy because she wanted to be difficult. Indeed, Kim's behavior wasn't a matter of choice.

Strictly speaking, there's no ego development of children at this stage. They haven't yet discovered themselves as persons separate from their mother. But in their development from birth to approximately age two, they'll learn trust, self-confidence, and self-determination as they discover they are unique individuals.

Babies Need Tough Parenting

Because the first five years are so important to our children's development, I devote more space to this period than to some of the later years. When we develop a pattern of tough parenting from the very beginning, not only do our children more readily accept it, but we also will find it easier to apply the principles of tough parenting throughout the rest of their development.

A newborn child isn't capable of decision making. Early behavior is primarily reflexive in response to survival needs. These reflexive responses are nature's way of helping a baby survive.

The Birth Struggle Long before people understand that adversity is a friend and that our determination to struggle and survive is essential to living, they instinctively engage in that struggle—in the birth process. *All* babies who make it through vaginal delivery experience minor trauma, and some even experience major trauma. In breech delivery (born bottom-first), nerves in the shoulder region can be injured, causing temporary paralysis of the arm. If vacuum extraction or forceps are used, your baby may sustain a prominent bruise to the scalp and experience temporary facial paralysis if the facial nerve is traumatized. Broken bones—the collarbone, upper-arm bone, and ribs—are another hazard of difficult delivery.

When doctors anticipate a difficult delivery, they often resort to Caesarean delivery. But they do so hesitantly because they know the baby runs the risk of having respiratory problems, particularly if the child is premature. It's as if nature is saying, "Yes, vaginal delivery is a terrible struggle, but it's the struggle that gives life!"

This is a foundational principle to tough parenting. Because it's the struggle that gives life, we must get out of the way and permit our children to engage in that struggle. Tough parenting doesn't permit the child to be defeated, and it helps if necessary. But it doesn't relieve the child of the struggle.

Think for a moment of what babies go through in their struggle to be born. They have been living in a state of absolute equilibrium and total comfort in the womb. Everything has been done for them. But the time comes when nature says, "Here's your first experience with disequilibrium!" The fact that it's called *labor* should give some clue as to what the baby is about to face!

The novice midwife may want to help, but the baby's head must not be touched until it's out. Even when the head is out, it shouldn't be pulled—just supported. The struggle is still the baby's struggle to get the shoulders out. Yes, the head and body need support, but the baby must act in concert with its mother's contractions.

Nature, here, offers us a remarkable metaphor: Life is a struggle from the day we are born. The struggle comes at its appointed time. It's necessary for the child to engage in the struggle. And we dare not attempt to delay the struggle or unnecessarily assist it because we'll damage the child. The struggle is essential to life, whether the child is going through the birth process or through subsequent stages of development.

Tough Parenting at Four Weeks Birth is a time of disequilibrium for babies. The comfort and stable environment of the womb is gone. Nature forces them to give up those comforts for a world of bright lights, heat and cold, noise, physical discomfort, and hunger.

Tough parenting for newborns involves our helping them achieve equilibrium by four weeks. We should expect their sleeping and waking patterns to become more definite. They should react positively to comfort and negatively to discomfort and be able to communicate these feelings to their parents. By four weeks they should establish a foothold in the world, a position of relative peace, a feeling that their needs are met.

Parents can facilitate bringing their babies to their first stage of equilibrium by understanding their needs and by learning how to communicate effectively with them. Though we can't communicate with words and ideas, we can communicate through the baby's sensory channels of hearing, seeing, and feeling. A mother's face and the soothing sounds of singing register on her baby as something pleasant.

Holding our babies and gently cuddling and rocking them are also pleasant experiences for them. Stroking their skin and gently massaging them makes touching a pleasant experience, which they later will consciously seek out.

Our babies can't *know* that we love them. But they can *experience* our love through their senses. We're nice to be around.

It's important for both mothers and fathers to communicate with their babies this way. Although mothers often have more opportunity to express security and love to their babies, it's equally important for babies to experience those expressions from their dads. Often, dads wait until their children develop more of a personality before they begin to get involved. They tend to think in terms of the things they're going to do *with* their children such as going to the zoo, playing ball, or fishing.

Dads already have something to do. It's to *make their children feel good through physical contact with them!* You need to begin to establish a feeling relationship with them from the beginning.

Tough Parenting at Sixteen Weeks When babies are between four and sixteen weeks old, they go through a period of disequilibrium. Nature will whisper in their ear, "It's time to find something more interesting to do." They no longer will be content to lie on their backs. They want to be held or propped up in a sitting position where they find more interesting things to see.

During this stage of development, babies will attempt to make their wants known, usually by crying. Sometimes they want to be picked up and cuddled, but no one responds to them. Other times, they've had enough stimulation and want to be left alone, but they can't get any peace and quiet.

This often is a time of frustration for both parents and their babies. Parents don't always know what the baby's cries mean. And even when they do understand the baby, other demands often keep them from meeting the baby's needs immediately. But this is what tough parenting is about. Parents need to accept their limitations and not feel guilty. Unhappiness with these situations forces babies to muster inner strength to cope, either by making their needs clearer or by accepting their situation.

Even if we could anticipate and meet all of our children's needs before they cry, we would only hinder their development by not letting them struggle. It's through the struggle to make themselves understood that they master communication with parents and develop a relationship to them.

This process reminds me of our relationship to God through prayer. God knows our needs even before we ask. But it's through the process of talking to him about our needs and thanking him for meeting our needs that we develop a relationship to him.

By sixteen weeks, things smooth out a bit for babies. They don't seem so helpless and squirmy. Their physical, or motor, skills have improved. Eating and sleeping patterns are more established. They follow objects with their eyes and reach out. And to our delight, they now make social contact by cooing and laughing.

It's important to recognize that all of these gains were made through the frustrations of disequilibrium. And though our children reach a stage of equilibrium at sixteen weeks, the next developmental stage will introduce new challenges and frustrations.

Coping at Twenty-Eight Weeks By age twenty-eight weeks, babies reach another plateau in their development. But again, not without frustration.

Between the ages of sixteen and twenty-eight weeks, nature again will nudge them. They'll become dissatisfied with their present level of achievement and start trying new things. They'll make their first moves at learning to crawl, but they won't be able to get on their knees. And they'll let us know they're frustrated. They'll try to sit alone, but they'll fall. They'll want to grasp things, only to find the pretty things elude them. And they'll cry when their mommy leaves.

Don't despair. This is a period of disequilibrium, and your children's behavior is normal. Their old skills are no longer adequate to meet their growing awareness of their world. Yet they don't have the new skills to match their new awareness. Be patient with them and encourage them to keep trying.

Remember that only *they* can develop those needed skills. And they can develop them only if their parents stand by and encourage them to master new skills on their own.

By the time babies are twenty-eight weeks old, new skills developed through trial and error begin to pay off and they seem more content. They reach another plateau of equilibrium, where they—and their parents—can catch their breath.

Our positive attitude is essential. It's an attitude that says, "Keep trying; you'll make it." Because our children trust us when we say they will make it, they keep on trying and succeed. And the positive developmental cycle continues.

Coping at Forty Weeks Forty weeks is another time of equilibrium. But disequilibrium comes first. Between ages twenty-eight and forty weeks, our children's awareness of their world continues to grow, and they again attempt to master their new world by developing new physical skills, accompanied by many frustrations. For example, their further attempts at crawling result in their going around in circles. But going around in circles is a frustration they'll experience again and again in life. They'll learn, however, that persistence and parental help and encouragement will enable them to achieve a new equilibrium. They'll be able to get up on all fours and crawl.

This period of disequilibrium will also bring new fears. The unfamiliar face of a stranger may bring tears and withdrawal. And yet getting used to an unfamiliar face is the price our babies pay for their new awareness of their surroundings. Our positive attitude that says, "You'll be okay," assures the baby that nothing's wrong. By forty weeks they learn that strangers are okay. But this growth comes only with struggle.

Tough parenting means that we accept the fears and tears, patiently bear with them, and encourage the baby to do the same. Remember, our children catch our attitudes long before they understand the words we say.

Tough Parenting at Fifty-Two Weeks As babies grow older, their development isn't as rapid. Between forty and fifty-two weeks they again show fear of strangers, but by fifty-two weeks they'll be sociable again. Tough parenting means that we permit our babies to experience these fears and tears, though we want to be sure that they're not overwhelmed by either. Remember that the baby is learning to trust us. We are responsible to assess just how much the baby can handle.

Most parents have enough good sense to know how much is too much. And when we miscalculate, babies let us know with their tears—tears that don't dry quickly. Remember, with babies, we can gauge their distress not by how loudly they cry but by how quickly they stop crying when we comfort them. Some babies scream at everything, so that's not always a good stress indicator.

A baby's new skills require new parental adjustments at each developmental stage. This is especially true when babies begin to walk. They start by holding on to furniture. Their new mobility requires that we child-proof the house and watch for hazards away from home. Place breakable items out of their reach, and allow babies to play only where they're not a danger to themselves or household furnishings.

When my oldest son started walking, we thought we had child-proofed his room. And we made sure he stayed in his room by putting a gate across the door. One day he was playing in his room when we heard a terrible crash. We ran to see what had happened and discovered that he had pulled out his dresser drawers and climbed them like a ladder, making the dresser top heavy. Only a miracle kept him from being crushed when the dresser fell over.

His bedroom was upstairs, so imagine our fright when on another day we discovered that he had gotten the window screen open and had thrown out his bottle, blanket, and toys. Why he didn't go out too, only God knows.

Yet another time he managed to knock a picture off the wall, break the glass, and cut himself on it. It was a small finger cut, but he smeared blood all over the room. When we came to check on him, the gory scene just about gave us heart failure.

Sometimes we handle our children's new mobility inappropriately. We permit them to play in non-child-proofed areas and then tell them, "No, don't touch; don't do that." Our children are just doing what comes naturally. They're not yet old enough to respect property and understand what's not an appropriate plaything. Everything is fair game. Being told not to touch things is a confusing message to the child of this age. It's like being told not to breathe.

We should be thoughtful when we're visiting friends or relatives. We shouldn't give our babies free run of the house and keep telling them no. Our children don't know any better, but we should. We shouldn't make our children unwelcome guests because of our poor judgment.

Tough parenting is tough on us as well as our children. It means that we need to be informed and thoughtful in the way we control our children, and that can be hard work. Parents don't realize that it is often *they*, and not their children, who make them pariahs.

Your Self-Centered Baby

Babies need an environment in which they are able to develop cognitive, physical/emotional, and social skills. They need to find out how their body works, who these other people are around them, and how to communicate with other people.

Be Permissive with Your Baby My caution about social sensitivity shouldn't deter parents from understanding their infants' need for an environment in which they can grow with a minimum of hindrance. Paradoxically, at this stage of our babies' development, parents need to be permissive in a way that may be inappropriate after they are six months old and certainly is inappropriate after age eighteen months. Though babies don't develop a sense of self until after they're eighteen months old, they do begin to discover after six months that they can control their mom and dad with tears.

Babies are egocentric. They're interested only in themselves. But their egocentricity is totally sensory. They don't know that their demands often run contrary to their parents' needs.

This egocentricity isn't a matter of choice. It's essential for survival. Their sucking, touching, and comforting needs are purely reflexive and must be indulged if babies are to develop normally.

Give them all the cuddling and affection they want. You won't "spoil" them with affection. And as much as possible, let them touch and explore whatever attracts their interest. If you have done a good job of child-proofing the house and if you are thoughtful about the feelings of others when you're away from home, you shouldn't have to say no too many times.

Later on in this chapter we'll look at special concerns, particularly crying and how to handle it without allowing the child to be manipulative. But we shouldn't let this concern keep us from meeting the baby's need to be held and rocked, to crawl and explore.

Don't Overstimulate Although we can't "spoil" babies with too much cuddling, we can overstimulate them. Parents who want to do a good job of encouraging the child's development of motor, language, and interpersonal skills will sometimes overstimulate the baby with too many new sights and sounds and too much physical activity. How

much is too much varies from baby to baby. Try this and
see if it works.

First, if your baby is fussy and you have tried every way
you know how to make him or her feel comfortable (food,
dry diaper, rocking), lower the level of light, noise, and
activity and see if this makes the baby more contented.
Second, ask yourself how much of a need you have to
hurry your child's development so you can bask in the glow
of an exceptional child. Your baby may feel overstimulated
and hurried because of *your* ego needs.

Build Trust As babies experience their needs being met,
they discover that one special person regularly meets their
needs, usually their mother. They learn to recognize her
by sight and sound. It is she who provides sensory comfort
and reduces sensory distress. Somewhere between ages
four to eight months mothers become all-important to
babies and tend to be the only person they trust.

The process of building trust between mother and child
is essential to our children's sense of well-being and their
ability to build trust in the future. After six to eight
months, babies begin to trust other people. When they
discover that *other people* besides mother provide sensory
comfort and relieve sensory distress, their base of security
is enlarged. They develop an important sense that *people
can be trusted*.

This sense of trust is foundational to our children's later
development. This trust, which our children learn as
infants and refine as they grow, enables them to weather
the disappointments of life without giving up. In later
months and years, though they may have times of hurt and
disappointment, there is an abiding confidence that someone will be there for them.

The development of trust has an important influence on
spiritual development as well. People who grow up in a

nontrusting environment find it difficult to trust God. So building trust in the early months of life has far-reaching implications in our children's total development.

Be Consistent Consistency in dealing with our children is an important element in building trust. Even though babies don't understand consistency, they experience a sense of security in their parents' consistent love, care, and presence. They learn very early in their lives that they can count on some things. Consistent parents can be trusted.

Bond Developing trust results in an attachment between mother and child, an attachment known as *bonding*. Bonding is one of the first interpersonal skills a person learns.

Although recent studies of monkeys and rats suggest that the mother's hormones make her more responsive to her baby at birth, the consensus is that experience, not biology, is the important factor in bonding. Unlike some animal babies, who immediately bond with the first moving object they see after their birth, human babies bond somewhere between ages five months and twelve months.

In the beginning, children explore the world away from their mother without fear because they know that she'll be there if they need her. With experience they learn that the world out there isn't so frightening and that they can make it without their mother. Paradoxically, knowing that she's there helps them later learn that they don't need her. It's normal human psychology to feel secure when we know we have a safe refuge to run to.

Women who work outside the home are concerned about the impact of their separation from their babies. The most critical period for bonding is ages four to eight months. If an infant's mother isn't available, the baby will bond with any loving caregiver and develop trust as a result of this experience. The working mother may find it heartbreaking to pick up her baby from the day-care location, only to see her baby cling to the caregiver. A working mother may be missing out on the experience of bonding with her baby, but babies aren't arrested in their development when they bond with someone other than their mother. In the days when extended families lived together (grandparents, aunts, uncles, cousins), babies often were lovingly cared for by many relatives other than their mother.

If the father is the primary caregiver, the baby will bond with him. But if he isn't, he should at least be a visible and active person in the child's life, getting involved in everyday activities such as feeding and diapering. Physical contact with the child helps the child become familiar with the father, whose role becomes more important and visible as the child grows older. Early contact also helps the father to feel from the beginning that he is, and always will be, an important part of the child's life.

Accept Differences in Your Babies It's natural for parents to respond warmly and positively to a cuddly, cooperative baby. And it's also somewhat normal to be irritated by a listless or squirmy baby who acts as if he or she prefers not to be touched. However, be careful not to overreact to unresponsive babies. Our priority must be to maximize *their* comfort level rather than to satisfy *our need* to have a responsive, cuddly baby.

Darryl didn't realize the long-term effect his early response to his second daughter would have on their relationship. Darryl's first daughter, Jan, always had been a robust, active person like himself. But from the beginning, Tammy, his second daughter, was different. Her birth was difficult and traumatic, and Darryl jumped to the conclusion that she would be sickly like her mother. Darryl told his wife, "Well, it looks as if Jan is going to be like me and Tammy is going to have a lot of problems like you."

As long as Darryl feels the way he does, he will send Tammy the message that he likes her sister, but he doesn't like her. Tammy probably never will know that from the moment of birth, she didn't have a chance with her dad just because she was sickly and reminded him of qualities he didn't like in her mother.

Other Parental Concerns

Parents have many questions and concerns about their babies in the first year. The two most common concerns are crying and teething.

Crying Why is the baby crying? What is the baby trying to communicate? Is it hunger? How long should we let the child cry? What if the baby doesn't cry?

Crying is the only way that babies can communicate with parents. If we listen carefully, we can distinguish different kinds of cries and nonverbal cues that go along with them.

For example, there's the fussy cry—the whimper. It's often accompanied by some movement of the arms and legs, but body movement isn't pronounced. Sometimes our babies are saying that they're not in terrible pain, but they're unhappy. This low-grade unhappiness often can be relieved by reducing light or noise, singing to them, patting their backs, or changing their position from back to belly (or reverse).

At the other extreme is the scream of pain, often accompanied by blotchy discolorations on the skin, emphasizing discomfort. Babies in acute pain will draw up their knees and then push down, suggesting that they may have stomach or intestinal distress. Infantile or three-month colic may be the problem. It occurs in one baby out of ten, starting at three or four weeks and ending at about twelve weeks. It's assumed that the problem is a spasm of the intestine, but its cause is unknown.

Some babies are comforted by rocking movements or by taking a ride in the car. Other babies find relief when they are placed on their stomach or on a warm washcloth and have their back stroked. Some babies settle down when they hear a constant, soothing noise like gentle music or the soft whirr of a fan or air conditioner.

Save your sanity by asking your spouse or other family members to help out. And remember, babies grow out of this stage. If you are tired or irritable, you won't be a source of comfort. Instead, impatience and rough handling will communicate negative, unsettling feelings to your baby.

Try not to feed babies when they're like this. They often get a bloated stomach and are more miserable. What's more, if we pop a bottle or pacifier into babies' mouths every time they cry, we condition them to connect discomfort with oral gratification. I often wonder how many of us are overweight adults for this very reason. We tend to deal with our physical and emotional discomfort with oral gratification. I don't rule out the use of a pacifier, but I suggest trying other methods of comfort first.

Though we can't spoil our babies with too much love, our need to attend to other household duties will mean that our babies will sometimes have to cope with discomfort on their own. We can't always pick them up every time they grunt, squirm, or fuss—and we don't need to. We have to sleep at night and so do our babies. If we make ourselves available to play late at night, they may come to expect it from us.

How long should we let our babies cry? In their first four to six weeks, we ought to respond to them immediately.

After that, if they're only fussing, see if they'll calm themselves.

How quickly they calm down after we comfort them is another indicator of how long we should let them fuss. If they calm down right away, we could have waited longer. If it takes longer than ninety seconds, pay attention a little sooner. This method of trial and error helps us learn which cries mean distress and which cries mean "It's time to party!"

My wife and I loved to play with Steve, our first son, when he was a baby. When we turned out the lights and went to bed, Steve often would cry, even though he was fed and dry. If we let it go for several minutes, he would grow louder and louder until he was screaming as if he felt pain.

I remember turning on the lights and going to his crib. But the minute he saw me, he stopped crying and flashed a big grin. I learned that Steve's screaming after lights out didn't mean he was in distress. So we let him cry, and he eventually settled down.

But this can create other problems. Sometimes children who cry for a long time will swallow a lot of air and then develop gas bubbles in their stomach. They'll continue to cry even when we try to console them. All a parent can do is "ride it out" with them. Eventually the crying will stop.

Parents who are too attentive to their babies' needs actually may encourage them to control the household with their tears. Yes, we should respond immediately to them in their first four to six weeks. But after that we should begin to let them calm themselves.

Teething At about three months, babies may begin to drool a great deal, have a low-grade fever (a degree or so above normal), and experience a loss of appetite. If they're uncomfortable, they'll let you know. The child's gums will be discolored or very swollen. A frozen teething ring will give some comfort and will help them get their teeth through the gums. However, if your baby has a temperature above 100.5°, consult your doctor and watch for infection.

The discomfort of teething and nature's demand on babies to accept it as part of the normal process of development provide us with another opportunity to practice tough parenting. Though we should attempt to make our babies comfortable, we shouldn't become overwrought because we can't relieve them of their distress. By going through discomfort, our babies learn to accept it as a normal part of development.

In times like these, your attitude is important. If, after you have done everything you can do to comfort your child, your attitude is, "This is normal, and it will pass," your children will learn to accept life's burdens and to muster their own inner strength to cope with them.

Summary

At birth, babies have normal reflexes that help in their development. In the early months, their actions and tears are their way of communicating their frustration at not getting what they want.

Before they are six months old, we need not worry about spoiling babies. But after six months, they can control us through their tears. We know that they're attempting to control us when our response to them immediately stops the tears. By not responding to babies under such circumstances, we condition them to trust that we'll be there for them but not to think that they can control us.

Yes, Alice, tough parenting is necessary for babies. When we and our babies accept the rigors of adversity from the beginning, we can be confident that we've made a good start.

3

Helping Your Baby Become
Self-Confident: Age One

At age one, babies face a new task: becoming self-confident. A new world is open to them. Their physical development enables them to move farther and faster than ever, and their mental development gives them a new awareness that piques their curiosity about everything. Their ability to master this new world has a profound effect on their self-confidence and makes them feel positive about trying to do new things—an attitude that lasts a lifetime.

But they also face a new conflict. For all of their short lives, they have been able to do what they have wanted. Now, even though they must have the opportunity to develop their self-confidence by exploring their new world and trying new things, they'll hear the word *no* with growing frequency. Their mothers, whom they have seen as an extension of themselves up to now, begin to emerge as separate people, who don't always give them what they want. In fact, mothers sometimes thwart their desires.

Here, then, is the parental task: We must help our one-year-olds develop self-confidence by permitting new and more complex activities, while at the same time we may need to curtail other activities either to protect them or because something more important needs to be done at the moment. For example, you're visiting at your friend's house with your one-year-old daughter who is fascinated with your friend's cat. Your daughter insists on picking up the cat despite your friend's warning that the cat is grouchy and sometimes bites.

You have a dilemma. On the one hand, you don't want to make your daughter afraid of animals. On the other hand, you have a responsibility to introduce her to hazardous situations carefully. Perhaps you could ask your friend to hold the cat while your daughter pets it, well away from the cat's mouth. Even under these circumstances, the cat may still snap at your daughter. But this may be a prudent risk to take for your daughter to learn that cats, though cute and cuddly, sometimes can be mean.

Helping one-year-olds develop self-confidence doesn't mean giving them the freedom to do whatever they want to do. But it does mean, as much as possible, to go along with their curiosity and their desire to try new things. Be prepared to guard them against permanently damaging risks, but don't be afraid to take prudent risks so your child will get the complete picture.

If the cat snaps at your daughter and even nicks her, it probably won't traumatize her, and it certainly won't permanently injure her. But of course, that's a father's view. I agree with Dr. Fitzhugh Dodson, in *How to Father*, that we fathers tend to permit more risk taking than mothers do.

Your Baby's Development at Age One

Things are a lot easier when babies stay in their cribs and are content with it. At age one, however, they are much more mobile and need freedom to move about to develop their large muscles.

One-year-olds crawl on hands and knees, pull up and walk by holding on to furniture. They may be able to walk with their mom or dad holding their hand. Their need to satisfy their curiosity and develop fine motor skills and eye-hand coordination means that they'll want to feed themselves or play with things while we're feeding them. This will make feeding more difficult and a bigger mess to clean up. But we must remember that one-year-olds don't understand the pressure we feel to get them fed, cleaned up, and off to bed so we can get on with other chores. They're doing their thing—practicing being a one-year-old.

What do we do with this pressure? Do we become impatient? Do we communicate to our children (verbally and nonverbally) that they're doing something wrong? Do we want to tell them they shouldn't practice being a one-year-old?

We must not expect our one-year-old to make it easy for us. We may have to allow more time for tasks such as bathing, feeding, and dressing in order to avoid the inevitable frustrations that come with trying to get the cooperation of a curious, active one-year-old.

Sometimes we can distract them by talking to them. Or we may need the other parent's help with the baby chores, particularly when both parents work outside the home and the morning schedule is so hectic.

Single parents will find that priorities have to be reordered, and a lot of things simply won't get done. The dishes will go undone some days. But come what may, though you'll feel annoyed that your children are more interested in their own wants than in yours, your understanding attitude will go a long way to keep every morning from being a battle with your baby.

One-year-olds are quick to pick up positive and negative feelings in people. Attitude and tone of voice convey to them how we're feeling. If we've done a good job with them in the early months, they'll feel that we're safe people to be around. They will have learned to trust us. If they pick up harshness in our attitude or tone of voice, they'll take it personally. They don't know that we're frustrated by other pressures.

Another irritation is their habit of throwing and dropping things. But this is the way they practice their motor skills and develop awareness. When we're trying to feed them, they're not being bad when they deliberately drop their bottle on the floor and then cry for us to pick it up. They're just doing the work of being one-year-olds. We may be trying to get ready for work, but they're already on the job.

Dads Are Important Too Helping our children develop self-confidence means giving them the opportunity to crawl, walk, climb, throw, pick things up, and play to their heart's content—without being a danger to themselves, others, or property. It may mean having to stand nearby to keep them from hurting themselves.

For example, if they try to climb up and down stairs, they run the risk of falling. It's better to let them try and catch them when they fall than to prevent them from trying at all. They'll get some bumps and bruises trying. But this is all part of learning their limits. And it also teaches them that bumps and bruises are a normal part of growing up. Tough parenting that has an accepting attitude toward these bumps and bruises helps the child to accept them too.

Dads are an important part of the process, given the tendency of some dads to be less protective than moms. I don't mean that they're careless; some dads simply tend to allow their children to take more chances. They can provide valuable opportunity for one-year-olds to stretch their skills.

Tough parenting means that we permit our kids to handle life's demands themselves as much as possible. The more they are permitted to do for themselves, the more able they are to develop the necessary skills to cope.

If, because of a pressing schedule, we get irritated and tell our children, "Here, let me do it," we make our children think it's not okay to try. They may fight us and adopt aggressiveness as their response to conflict. Or they may give up, become too docile, and adopt passivity as their way of handling conflict in life.

The same is true when we repeatedly tell our children, "Don't do that. You'll hurt yourself." But if we permit our children (within reason) to get themselves in trouble and get a little scared or hurt, they're much more likely to be careful the next time and develop the necessary skills to keep from getting hurt.

Another place where dads can make a unique contribution is in rough-and-tumble play. Dads tend to be more vigorous in play than moms are. This is especially important for the very active child who needs more activity for physical and emotional development. Sometimes children who don't seem content need more vigorous activity. One caution, however: Don't play roughly just before mealtime or bedtime. Give children time to settle down so they'll be ready to eat and sleep.

A *Question of Quality Time* Families today face a dilemma

that requires our understanding. Though the ideal of family life may be a stay-at-home mom who is baking cookies when the kids come home from school, social realities don't always permit it.

Economic demands often require both parents to work outside the home, and the high incidence of divorce has produced many single-parent households, ninety percent of which are headed by a single mother who is barely able to keep up with the demands of supporting her child and meeting her own needs. Many parents have resorted to what they call "quality time," brief periods of structured activity with their children to make up for the lack of extended periods of unstructured time that parents might otherwise wish to spend with their children.

History teaches us that our dilemma isn't new. Before the industrial revolution, mothers worked at home, but they helped run the farm and often were not available to care for their children. They had to depend on extended family, such as an aunt or grandmother or the child's cousins. The child got a lot of love and good care from an extended family. Urban families often had a live-in nanny who did the same thing.

Though it's not ideal, it's okay for someone other than parents to give children love and an atmosphere in which they can develop self-confidence with patient adult oversight. We just need to be sure that we know what our children's developmental needs are and that those needs are met by caregivers.

One-year-olds need the primary caregiver to be around a great deal. Though we may have our "quality time" with our children, we must not suppose that it's a substitute for quality care that provides them with lots of exposure to a loving adult. One-year-olds' courage to explore the world around them is facilitated by the knowledge that a trusted adult is nearby. They want to be sure that they have a safe place to run to if things get too scary.

A hired caregiver, not the parent, may be that most trusted adult. This means that the caregiver understands our children's developmental needs, is willing to handle the children's attachment and detachment patiently, and is consistently part of their lives. If we parents can't be the primary caregiver, then we should be sure that our children have the same caregiver day in and day out. Too much change at this time of our children's lives may slow their development. They may be preoccupied with finding someone they can trust rather than getting on with the job of conquering their new and larger world.

Between Ages Eighteen Months and Two Years

By the time they are eighteen months old, most children are able to walk well, climb stairs with one hand held, crawl backwards down stairs, and stoop to pick up things. They have a vocabulary of six to twenty words and enjoy looking at picture books.

All of these developmental tasks may run in direct conflict with parental needs simply because of the time required to supervise and encourage our children. And if we aren't aware of our children's needs, we may unwittingly thwart their normal development.

Tough parenting *requires* us to understand not only our child's development but also how we can encourage it. This involves a consistent adult presence.

Scribbling Children love to scribble. If they find a crayon, pencil, or pen, they'll scribble on anything—walls, floors, furniture, themselves, maybe even paper!

Here we have an opportunity to set limits. We should tell them, "No, don't scribble on the wall. Here, scribble on this pad of paper." Notice that this approach not only establishes a limit but also suggests an alternative. Children learn by trial and error, and they'll make unnecessary mistakes unless they are told and shown what to do.

Scribbling is important to the development of fine motor skills and coordination. Children learn to hold a writing instrument. Scribbling also helps young children develop a sense of direction and how things move. They begin to understand that things don't just go, but they go in different directions. Things move up and down, left and right, forward and backward. Because they understand this, they are able to decide the direction they want to move. At this point they begin to learn which is their left and right side, and they begin to show a preference for right- or left-handedness. This kind of discrimination is essential to the development of reading and writing skills. It will later enable them to understand the difference between *b* and *d* and give them the ability to move their crayon to make a *b* or *d*. Scribbling is the first step in developing the primary skill of writing language—making marks that mean something.

Scribbling can be another one of those messy, time-consuming developmental tasks, but it's an essential task. Tough parenting sometimes is tough on us. It demands that we be informed and patient with our children.

Shoes and Socks Another developmental task related to our children's fine motor skill and eye-hand coordination is putting on shoes and socks. How often have we had the experience of getting our children all dressed only to come back and find that they've taken off their shoes and socks and are trying to put them back on again?

We sometimes may feel that they're trying to make life more difficult for us. But our children have made a new discovery. These things on their feet called shoes and socks are put on and taken off, and nature is nudging them to try it themselves. They may not understand our telling them, "Let's do that later." And we won't like it when they resist our attempts to put the shoes and socks back on. Just remember: They're not deliberately being difficult; they are developing essential skills.

I'm not suggesting that we always give in to our children. We may have to say, "No, now isn't a good time." The key is our *attitude* as parents—one that says, "I understand that you don't like this. We'll have to do this later, when the time is right." Then we must make sure that we *do* take time later.

A caring attitude tells our children that they're okay and what they want is okay, but not right now. When gratification of their wants and needs is put off, they learn a lesson in the development of their social skills. These little people who have been self-centered all of their lives begin to learn that they can't always have things the way they want, when they want. It has nothing to do with their "okayness" or the "okayness" of what they want.

Conflict of the Wills

Conflict between our needs and our children's needs is a major battle we are going to have with our children. This conflict starts at approximately eighteen months and will last until they move out on their own. How intense the conflict gets, how we deal with it, and when we get a reprieve will vary throughout the developmental stages. The first round of conflict of the wills begins at age eighteen months and lasts until age five or six.

Though our children at eighteen months are discovering their world and are beginning to assign names for their parents and perhaps their bottle or blanket, they don't think of objects as separate from themselves. They view everything as an extension of themselves and, therefore, as something they have a legitimate claim on. The idea of *mine* as opposed to *yours*, and *me* as opposed to *you*, is a foreign idea.

Even after children begin to make this differentiation at age two, they still are very egocentric. They think that the world actually is as *they* perceive it. But over the years, their version of reality will be challenged. By the time they are five or six years old, they'll conclude that there is a version of reality apart from what they understand it to be and that *someone else may have a clearer view of things.* This realization occurs when they begin to understand abstract thinking. They are able to step out of the egocentric world of their own experience into the real world, and they are able to learn new things that are unrelated to their experience and the way they view things.

This is important to understand because our children at age eighteen months aren't being stubborn when they insist that their view or their way is correct. They have an immature view of the world. This doesn't mean that the child's view shouldn't be corrected. But we should deal with them as immature children who have an immature view of life rather than as children who are determined to be difficult.

Summary

Developing self-confidence is our children's major developmental task at age one. They do this by trying new things such as feeding themselves, climbing, and exploring with a trusted adult standing nearby to rescue them if necessary.

An important part of their development at this age is to learn that their wants usually are okay, but that they might not be able to have what they want whenever they want it. They realize that their mom and dad are going to start setting limits on them.

Setting Limits at Age Eighteen Months

Parents who don't correctly assess their children's maturity may find it difficult to set limits. For example, parents who leave breakable objects around the house, expecting their eighteen-month-old not to touch them, fail to recognize their child's developmental stage. Touching these things is part of the developmental task, and children who do touch aren't being bad. The wisest way to set limits is to remove breakable objects and close off inappropriate areas with gates or doors.

Though I believe in appropriate spanking (see chapter 4), it's not usually necessary to spank an eighteen-month-old. I say *usually* because if children run out into the street or engage in other life-threatening behavior, we may need to get their attention with a good swat on the rear end. But there are other ways to set limits.

Physical Control Children at this age usually are small enough to control physically by picking them up and putting them where they refuse to go. And if it's a battle of the wills, we may need to do it in a way that underscores our determination—firmly and with a no-nonsense attitude.

God gives us children in small packages to allow us plenty of time to bring them under control when necessary. It's no accident that we're bigger than they are until it's time for them to leave home.

When we exercise our power, it's important that we show our determination to exercise it until our children give in. If we exercise our power halfheartedly, our children will see it as weakness and continue to buck us until we give in. Or if we give in to their repeated challenge of our power, we'll teach them to fight until we give in.

Single parents and parents who are burdened with too much to do often lose the battle at this point. They don't invest the necessary time or energy to set limits and stick with them. As a consequence, their children don't take them seriously.

Sometimes single parents have a misguided notion of kindness. Feeling that their children have suffered enough with the losses and displacement of divorce or death, they don't want their children to face more disappointment by being told no. Exactly the opposite is true. Children of divorce need to feel that the custodial parent is able to pick up the pieces and carry on. Parents who aren't as firm after divorce or death of a spouse raise a serious question in the minds of their children about their ability to parent.

Single parents' hesitance to set limits often prompts children to misbehave or push limits as a way of testing to see how much control the parent has. The purpose of the test isn't to gain more freedom but to be sure that someone is in charge.

Reduce the Demands on Your Child Parents who are in constant conflict with their children may need to reduce the number of demands they make of them. Sometimes we must decide what is most important and let everything else go.

For example, most of us like a tidy house. But children have a way of dragging out all of their toys and scattering them throughout the house. *Must* you have all the toys picked up by bedtime or by work the next day? Maybe you would be better off meeting your own (or your child's) immediate needs and setting a cleanup time the next day.

Another way of handling clutter is to reduce our children's play area and the amount of toys they can scatter. Most American children have too many things, and toys just become part of the household clutter. Put some toys away for a time, and later on take them out and put others away. The out-of-sight toys will be new and interesting once again.

Natural Consequences Natural consequences are a good way for children to learn limits. Say, for example, your son is determined to climb out of his playpen and screams if you try to prevent him. But if he is allowed to fall once or twice and suffer a minor bump or bruise, he'll not be so determined the next time. It's important for parents to stand by and be sure he doesn't do a Humpty-Dumpty and crack his head open. But the hard knocks of life are an excellent way of helping him learn his limits.

Natural consequences can be used with children who run away when we're trying to get our shopping done. It may help to let them run away and think that they're lost (as we watch out of the corner of our eye). Their own resulting fear will probably cause them to stay nearby for the rest of the shopping trip.

Other Parental Concerns

Every stage of development presents special concerns. Parents of one-year-olds are typically concerned about toilet training, weaning, comforting habits, and day care.

Toilet Training I would prefer to introduce this subject later in the developmental process, but because I run into a significant number of parents who tend to hurry their children, I will deal with it here. Some parents take a great deal of pride in having their children achieve toilet training by the time they are one year old—a very questionable practice. The very earliest we should even try bowel training is when the child is eighteen months old. Bladder training comes later—for good reasons.

First of all, a child's nervous system must be sufficiently mature to control the sphincter muscles. Second, children must be old enough to understand a complex learning task.

Bowel movements occur naturally when the colon slumps toward the rectum, producing pressure on the rectum. The child's natural reflex is to relax the sphincter and strain the abdominal muscles to evacuate the bowel.

Bowel training requires us to teach our children to change the way they handle this urge. Rather than relax the sphincter, children are encouraged to tighten it. Children must be physically developed enough to do this and cognitively developed enough to understand what we want. And they must do all this while they walk to the bathroom, pull down their pants, and sit on the potty! That's a lot for a child to do. And that's why toilet training should wait for at least another year.

Weaning Sometimes parents rush weaning as they do toilet training because they have a need to boast about their precocious child. No scientific evidence suggests that your child will become a brain surgeon or senator because he or she has been toilet trained or weaned before the rest of the kids in the neighborhood. In fact, when you rush your child, you tell a lot more about yourself than about your child.

We should pace our children's progress according to their timetable, not ours. Children who develop normally don't feel overwhelmed by parental demands for progress.

Children are born with the sucking reflex to assure their ability to get food following birth. But somewhere between three and six months, babies begin to eat pureed food and become less dependent on the sucking reflex.

As our children grow older, sucking becomes less an eating necessity and more a comfortable association with the past. Some children need this comfort more than others and may need to be deprived gradually of their bottle or their mother's breast. Children may accept the fact that they can have their bottle only before nap and bedtime, and after a while only before bedtime. But eventually the bedtime bottle will have to go.

When do we wean? The guiding rule should be a sensitivity to your child's feelings of security. My wife and I realized that our oldest son, Steve, as a high-energy child, needed a greater feeling of security than our second son, Dave, who was quieter, less demanding, and more secure. Steve got a lot of security out of his bottle.

When Dave began to show little interest in his bedtime bottle at fourteen months, we decided to wean him and Steve at the same time. Steve was two years old.

Dave made no fuss for his bedtime bottle, but Steve acted like a junkie needing a fix. I decided that I would help him through withdrawal by staying up with him, all night if necessary.

Whenever Steve would cry pitifully for his bottle, I would rock or pat him until he calmed down. I knew that he needed comforting, but he would have to get it from rocking and patting, not his bottle.

When he would drift off to sleep, I would put him down and read, knowing that it would be just a matter of time before he would be looking for his bottle again. After a night without his bottle, he accepted the idea that he could do without it. He had some wakeful spells, but patting him got him back to sleep.

Giving up the comfort of his bottle was a major step of growth for Steve and shows why coping should be viewed as a natural part of the developmental process. We shouldn't act as if adversity is a stranger or think that we can somehow relieve our children of life's unpleasantness. We can't, and we shouldn't try. But we can be there for them while they're struggling with it and lend our comfort and support. When ordinary demands of life are handled this way, our children are prepared to handle the extraordinary demands the same way. They accept the demand to cope as usual rather than unusual, and they find comfort and support from those who love them.

Comforting Habits Comforting habits are closely related to the comfort of the bottle or breast. Though the need for the sucking reflex quickly disappears, it still is a source of comfort transferred to the thumb or an object such as a blanket or stuffed animal.

Some comforting habits seem bizarre to parents. Sometimes children will rock themselves and bang their heads against the crib as they rock. There's nothing odd about such behavior, and if the banging bothers you, just pad the crib so the sound doesn't irritate you and the child doesn't get hurt.

Children eventually give up their comforting habits and security blankets. But it's often difficult to keep security blankets clean and in good repair because children object to your tampering with their blankets, which don't feel or smell the same after being washed.

Comforting habits and security objects help children make a transition from the comfort of a mother's touch to providing for their own comfort. How and why children choose their security objects often defies an explanation. Children have been known to choose a pot holder, a painting, or a vacuum cleaner.

Most children give up their security objects by age five, though they may use them from time to time when they feel sick or insecure. Sometimes peer pressure, like being called a baby, makes them decide to give up their security object.

The pressures of life force our children to grow up and cope in more mature ways. We can facilitate these transitions by being matter-of-fact and letting our children feel the pressure from others to give up immature behavior.

Day Care Working parents often feel caught in a bind between the need to work outside the home and the need to provide adequate care for their children. Here are some pointers.

First of all, there's nothing wrong with having someone other than the parent care for a child. It's been done for centuries, when the clan was a societal unit and relatives took care of the young. In some homes today families have live-in nannies or tutors.

Both mother and child would benefit by having the first eighteen months together. This is a time of bonding (birth to age one) and a time when children need a familiar and trusted adult nearby to encourage the development of self-confidence and to protect them when they feel insecure.

If a stand-in parent is needed, he or she must be able to meet three needs the child has.

1. *Children need to be loved and to belong to a family.* Even the infant in the crib needs to be picked up and loved. The warm touch of the caregiver communicates a feeling of belonging.

2. *Children need specific information.* They need to know colors, numbers, and words, and most important, how to gather information without help. This is essential to developing maturity, independence, and self-confidence. This means that young children need to be in smaller groups so they may interact more with the adult caregivers.

3. *Children need rules for interacting with each other.* In one study of children who had been in day care from ages six weeks to five years, their behavior showed fifteen times more aggressiveness than in a control group. Adequate adult interaction early in the child's life is essential for the child to learn kindness, nonaggressive behavior, and task persistence. Caregivers who remind children of the rules of behavior at the time of an aggressive act and do so sternly in a one-on-one interaction help children to show kindness as they grow older.

Parents can do several things to ensure a positive day-care experience.

1. *Check the caregiver/child ratio.* Before enrolling your child, be sure that the ratio of caregivers is adequate for the child population: no more than four babies per caregiver, five to six toddlers per caregiver, and with children over age three, one caregiver per seven children. Smaller groups permit more personal attention. Be sure the caregivers are devoted to the children and are supervised adequately so the children are getting the benefit of the care. Caregivers should be hired on a review basis, which means that their employment depends on their passing a periodic review, the first one being no more than six weeks after employment.

2. *Check the quality of care.* Be sure that quality day care is maintained after the child is enrolled. It's also important to have the same caregiver available for the children so that rules for social conduct may be set and followed consistently. Those who supervise caregivers must enforce the rule that the caregivers don't socialize with each other during working hours. Their attention is to be devoted to the children. Even nap time is an occasion for the caregiver to observe the children and spot any troubled

behavior patterns such as repeated failure to obey rules, disturbed sleep, or bed-wetting. Ask questions: Is the caregiver/child ratio maintained? Are the caregivers adequately supervised?

3. *Assess the atmosphere.* Ask for permission to visit the day-care center so you can familiarize yourself with what a child does during the day. You may need to do it when your child is taking a nap because your presence may be disruptive to your child and to the program. Get involved with your day-care center to make the atmosphere as caring as possible toward the children. The physical plant and activities should be homelike. Activities should stimulate interaction between the caregivers and the children. The mood of interaction, even in discipline, should show loving concern.

4. *Give your child quality time.* When you are with your child, make your time count. That is difficult with preschool children because of their limited attention span. Teaching a child of this age is responsive rather than directive. This means that a parent takes advantage of situations that lead to learning experiences—conflict with another child, disappointment over the weather, or the loss of a prized possession. Sometimes household tasks must be interrupted or even suspended to capitalize on a teaching opportunity.

Television doesn't offer this kind of opportunity simply because the television story moves on, and a parent doesn't have time to stop and explain. It's important to offer simple commentary while children watch television. When they see people on television behaving in a criminal or antisocial manner and don't understand motives or consequences, they are missing an important lesson. If they don't understand the real consequences of such behavior, they may want to copy the behavior because it looks exciting.

Reading with the child is a better activity. Talking about the pictures and story gives the parent an opportunity to connect these things to the child's everyday world.

5. *Connect home and day care for the child.* When a child is only a year old, it's difficult for a parent to know how the day went at the day-care center. We should know the program and the day-care workers well enough that we can talk to our child about what goes on during the day. Do at home some of the same activities your child does at the day-care facility so the child has a sense of continuity.

Christian parents will want to explore the possibility of putting their children in a Christian day-care center. If the center is a part of your church, it may be a bonus because the child is already familiar with the surroundings. The Christian outlook and atmosphere may also make it less likely for parents to run into ideological conflicts with the caregivers.

Be sure that the facilities and staff meet the criteria described above. And remember that Christian caregivers aren't flawless people. Don't be less vigilant in monitoring the care facility just because it's Christian.

4

Taming the Terrible Twos:
Age Two

The terrible twos are legendary, and for good reason. As babies, children are naturally self-centered: it's essential to their survival. Between ages one and two, they learn to become more self-confident children. At age two they discover that they are individuals and not an extension of their mother. It's only natural then that having made this discovery, this self-centered, self-confident child attempts to become self-determined.

As with all other new discoveries, self-determination is a concept children must try out to see if it really works. If they really are people distinct from their parents, they should be able to assert their own will in opposition to their parents' will.

Parents are confronted with a difficult task. On one hand, we want to reinforce this new development. But we also need to teach our children about *social skills*. Though they may assert their will independently of others, sometimes it's not a wise thing to do. Our children need to learn that getting their way isn't the most important thing in life. They must learn that yielding to the wishes of other people sometimes is best.

This is a lesson we'll have to teach our children again and again until they leave home. They must find the balance between self-determination and being a cooperative member of society.

Who's in Charge?

When our children are small, we're pretty much able to control them physically. For example, if we have been fair and reasonable about bedtime and our children still resist, we can pick them up and carry them to bed and make sure they stay there. But two-year-olds are beginning to get too big to lug around. How do we control our children then? Is physical control no longer an option?

Can You Reason with a Two-Year-Old? Some parents believe that it's time to begin to reason with the child. We certainly ought to encourage the development of cognitive and verbal skills. But at age two, the cognitive processes aren't sufficiently developed to enable us to reason successfully with the child. In fact, children at this age *can't* conceive that things ought to be any other way than their way.

It's also difficult to reason with two-year-olds because they are unable to distinguish their thoughts from their feelings or their wants from their needs. Our task as adults is to help them understand that their felt needs may be legitimate but that they can't always get what they want. Getting what they want may stand in the way of other people getting what *they* want, for instance.

When my grandson Jeremy was two years old, my wife and I spent a weekend taking care of him. I was watching the news on television when Jeremy came into the room and changed the channel so he could play with his Nintendo game. When I objected and told him I was watching the news, he just shrugged his shoulders and continued to play.

This called for tough parenting. Jeremy had to learn an important rule of social behavior—be considerate of other people's needs when fulfilling your own needs.

I asked Jeremy to stop playing his game and talk with me about what happened. But he didn't want to hear that his behavior was impolite, and he didn't want to talk about how we both could have our needs met. He got huffy and walked out of the room.

Parents of two-year-olds will recognize this behavior. I call my response to it tough parenting because we can't avoid confronting our children in ways that help them get on with the developmental task. Dealing with the same behaviors over and over can be tiring and irritating. But we must remember that two-year-olds do what comes naturally. And though our social sensibilities may be outraged by their self-centered, self-determined behavior, a consistent challenge of this behavior helps two-year-olds learn.

The Parental Mandate It doesn't take parents long to discover that no matter how reasonable, thoughtful, and gentle they are in dealing with their two-year-olds, they often are confronted with an attitude that defies their best efforts to guide their children gently. It's an attitude that says, "I'm going to do what I want, when I want, and you can't do anything about it."

If your two-year-old has never behaved like this, you are a most fortunate parent. But most parents have to deal with this problem. It helps to know that children do this not because they are inflexible but because they are testing their limits, seeing how far they can go in their quest to be a self-determined person.

Children who defy their parents need to know that society has order and parents have a *parental mandate*. In short, someone has to be in charge of family life. Though the mandate ought to be discharged intelligently and lovingly, it gives parents the last word in matters of family life. Yes, we understand what our children want, and we do our best to accommodate their wishes with an eye toward their overall development and health. But many times the child's wishes will be denied because parental wisdom sees that it's not in the child's or the family's best interest.

A well-ordered society has the right to expect parents to accept that mandate and enforce it as necessary to ensure stable family life. Treating children this way will enable them to fit into a society in which teachers, bosses, police officers, and government lawmakers also act according to a mandate.

Family life and social stability have suffered in recent years because we who have the mandate to maintain order aren't keeping order. And one reason we don't keep order is that we don't understand the seriousness of a challenge to that mandate.

When parents allow their two-year-olds repeatedly to be rude to adults and abusive to peers with no consequences for their behavior, they are failing to exercise the mandate. And in doing so, they risk encouraging their children to become even more antisocial in their behavior.

Parents usually are able to settle differences with their children by simple negotiation. I would have been happy to have turned over the television to Jeremy in five minutes when the news was over. But when a child insists on having his or her way in spite of parental good will or against parental good judgment, we must understand that an important shift in the issues has occurred.

The issue now is a challenge to the parental mandate. Do parents have the right to insist that a child is going to stop behaving in an unacceptable manner? A well-ordered home and properly socialized children hinge on this issue. When children successfully challenge their parents' ability to control their behavior, the parental mandate weakens and chaos results. We turn the home over to our children who have demonstrated that it is they, not their parents, who are in charge.

What About Spanking? How, then, do we control children who are too big to restrain physically? Is spanking a legitimate deterrent?

Spanking ought to be employed only as a last resort and only when the parental mandate is challenged. Some children have a temperament that responds without spanking. Their desire to please and our ability to control with other measures may obviate spanking. But not all parents have children who are that compliant. What then?

I suggest judicious spanking. Some parents will object, for one of several reasons.

Objection #1: Spanking is barbaric. Someone will say, "I don't know what the alternative is, but the idea of deliberately inflicting physical pain on another human being is unenlightened at best and barbaric at worst." I understand this response, but even though you may not spank, you'll find that pain does have its place in the developmental process. Let me explain.

I have already pointed out that we should permit our children to experience the pain of adversity in the interest of character development. They also will experience both emotional and physical pain from their failure to control their self-determination. This pain results when children experience the *natural consequences* of an inappropriate action, as I described in the previous chapter.

Natural consequences face our two-year-olds everywhere. Even though they are told to stay away from a hot stove, they get burned when they don't listen and touch it. Though they are told to keep their seatbelt fastened in the car, they sometimes disobey and are hurt when the driver slams on the brakes. They are told not to wander off in the store but are frightened back into obedience when they are careless and get lost.

Physical pain is part of the natural order that catches up with children who think they can't be stopped in their exercise of self-determination. It's a built-in corrective that removes from society those who violate the natural order. This is the plain meaning of the apostle Paul's warning to the Ephesians: "Children, obey your parents in the Lord, for this is right. 'Honor your father and mother'—which is the first commandment with a promise—'that it may go well with you and that you may enjoy long life on the earth'" (Eph. 6:1–3).

Self-determined children who will not obey their parents or respect the parental mandate will eventually experience the pain of natural consequences! In other words, our children are already experiencing the divinely ordained pain of natural consequences. Spanking, when employed judiciously, is another kind of pain that can help children learn their limits. As the proverb says, "Folly is bound up in the heart of a child, but the rod of discipline will drive it far from him" (Prov. 22:15).

Objection #2: Spanking teaches children to hit. Parents sometimes object to spanking because, they say, it teaches our children that it's okay to hit. But I don't think this is a sound position to take. If the parental mandate and the mandate of government are legitimate concepts, then we can't compare what a child does with what a parent or the government does. We who are charged with keeping order must have the right to deal out punishment as a way of making disobedience too costly for the uncooperative.

The manner in which punishment is meted out by the guardians of order also is different. It can't be compared to a child's hitting, hurting, or otherwise damaging others. The child who hurts others strikes out in anger and self-interest. Parents, on the other hand, must spank with a cool head and never in anger. If we can't do it with a cool head, we ought not to do it at all.

We must send the message to the child, "I'm spanking you because I'm responsible to make you understand that I'm in charge here, and bucking my authority will eventually cause you a great deal of pain—either from spanking or from other natural consequences. I need to give you a good reason to cooperate because all other attempts to gain your cooperation have failed."

We can say, "I love you too much to let you act like this. Everybody has to obey rules or be punished for breaking them. If you don't learn this now, you'll have a hard time following rules when you grow up. And when grownups break the rules, the punishment is a lot worse." A little pain for our children now (and for the parents who spank) may help them avoid a lot of pain later.

Not only must we avoid spanking in anger, we must spank in a way that doesn't cause physical harm. The child who hits doesn't care that hitting damages someone else. The parent who spanks does care and takes precautions not to damage the child. I recommend using a switch or a belt rather than the hand, paddle, or hair brush. A hand is heavy and bony and can give a child whiplash; a paddle or hair brush can hurt bones if our aim isn't good. A switch or belt will sting, but is less likely to damage. Whatever you choose, use the same instrument whenever possible for consistency's sake.

Because society has become so soft in dealing with offenders, spanking is regarded by many as child abuse. And no doubt, in some cases, it really is child abuse because parents lash out in anger and hit the child anywhere they want. But concern over child abuse puts in jeopardy parents who would control their children.

Objection #3: Spanking isn't loving. Some parents feel that inflicting the pain of spanking is foreign to the idea of love. I'm assured by the proverb that says, "My son, do not despise the LORD's discipline and do not resent his rebuke, because the LORD disciplines those he loves, as a father the son he delights in" (Prov. 3:11–12).

Television Viewing

Watching television need not be harmful to our children if viewing is monitored carefully. Let me suggest four guidelines for use of television with children of all ages.

1. *Know what your kids are watching.* The way the subject matter is presented is as important as the subject itself. For example, Mr. Rogers, in his typically gentle, tasteful manner, once read to his young audience a short book he wrote about toilet training—it was far more appropriate than a family sitcom in which parents and kids exchange barbs. We can help our kids be selective by commenting positively on programs that reflect our family's value system, by not laughing at fresh kids on family sitcoms, and by turning off the television if a program is inappropriate.

2. *Limit your children's time in front of the television.* The amount of television our kids watch affects their sense of

reality. The more time they spend in the television fantasy world, the larger and more real that world becomes.

3. *Watch television with your children.* Watch programs with them and talk about the show. Ask if your family acts the way the television family acts. Do you sound like the parents on the show? Do the kids act and talk like the kids on the show? You probably will find that when you talk about shows that don't measure up to the standards you want for your own family, the kids tend to watch something else.

4. *Find trustworthy programs.* When supervising your children's viewing, look for names you can trust, such as *Sesame Street* (PBS), *Mister Rogers' Neighborhood* (PBS), *Reading Rainbow* (PBS), *Shining Time Station* (PBS), *Storybook Classics* (Showtime), *Welcome to Pooh Corner* (The Disney Channel), and *Jim Henson's Muppet Babies* (CBS Syndication).

Television for Children Ages Two Through Five I have some special concerns for young children who watch television. Consider these issues when you allow children ages two through five to watch television.

1. *Action.* Children in this age group enjoy action. You may need to decide what action is acceptable and what is not. For example, many cartoons use slapstick comedy. Daffy Duck may hit Elmer Fudd over the head with a gigantic mallet, and Elmer may respond by getting his shotgun. Some parents see this as unacceptable violence. Others don't.

2. *Marketing.* Watch out for toy marketing under the name of animated cartoons. The cartoons promote the sale of

action figures or toys. New federal laws are designed to curtail this practice, but be alert to it.

3. *Violence*. Watch out for shows that always resort to fighting as a way to solve problems. Superhero stories usually have this theme. If you don't want to keep your children from seeing their favorite superhero, watch the show with them and suggest other ways to solve the problem. Remember, though, that superheroes stamp out evil, and we want to be positive about that.

Toilet Training

Bowel training An important feature of bowel training is the awareness of when your child is having a bowel movement and to capitalize on the natural slumping of the bowel. Bowels usually move around the same time every day, so keep alert and be prepared.

The first step in training is to call the child's attention to what's happening. Say to Joey, "Joey's having a BM." He must understand what a BM is and what it feels like before he can change his habit.

The second step is to put a potty chair in the bathroom and explain what it's for. You can show Joey that he is to pull down his pants and sit on the chair. A chair is preferable to a seat on the toilet because it's more accessible.

The third step is to *capitalize on the natural urge to evacuate the bowel*. Don't put Joey on the potty chair at your convenience. This confuses him. He's being expected to perform something he can't do. And if disapproval is connected with his failure to perform, it can undermine his self-confidence.

If we know when Joey's bowels usually move, we can put him on the potty before he begins. Even if he has already started, let him finish on the chair. But be sure that he isn't frightened by your insistence that he hurry to get on the chair.

Never force children to stay on the potty, and be prepared for accidents. When there is an accident, *don't scold!*

When we become impatient, we give children two things to worry about. Their first worry is, "I don't know what my mommy wants." The second worry is, "If I don't do what she wants, I'll be scolded." We create performance anxiety in our children whenever we send the message that it's not okay to fail.

We may help our children by showing them that the feces go in the potty. And don't be discouraged, as one mother was, when her child became very adept at doing his BM in his pants and then emptying it into the potty chair. He eventually got the idea that he could save time by going directly to the potty.

Our child is still developing self-confidence, and we help with a positive attitude that says, "I know you can do it," an attitude that is not disapproving when the child fails.

Bladder training Bladder training is harder to achieve than bowel training, mainly because the sensation to urinate isn't as dramatic as the urge to evacuate the bowel. Children go through three stages in learning how to urinate.

The first stage is helping them become aware that they are wet. We can make them aware by checking their diaper and letting them feel with their hand what wet means. Seeing their dad or brother urinate may help boys connect the idea of wetting with the potty chair. With little girls it may be more difficult because they're not able to see what's happening when their mommy urinates.

The second stage is making them aware of the fact that they are in the *process* of wetting. Training pants may be messy, and we may want to corral our children where they can't damage anything by getting it wet, but training pants allow enough leakage for them to see when they're wetting. When this happens, take them to the potty chair, and connect the idea of wetting with urinating in the potty chair.

The third stage is to help children be aware of when they are *about* to wet. If we've been observing them closely, we'll be aware of distress signals—that they're about to wet. We can then say, "Do you need to wet in the potty?" and then take them to the potty. The child may not void the bladder in the potty and may do it later in the training pants. When this happens, take the child back to the potty and say, "Wet in the potty."

Giving them approval for their success is as important as avoiding condemnation for their failure. Remember, we're attempting to develop self-confidence.

Sexual Awareness and Toilet Training Toilet training acquaints our children with their sex organs. They should learn the proper name for the penis or vulva and also the proper name for the process of elimination. Using the word *wet* rather than *urinate* is easier for them to handle. *BM* is quite adequate for bowel movement.

I realized I had failed to do this when my oldest son was a toddler. He was suffering from a painful rash on his penis and complained that his tail hurt.

But then again, I didn't feel too bad about my lack of instruction when my first and second sons called their feces, "do more." They inadvertently picked this up through potty training. When they did something in the potty, my wife or I would ask, "Do you have to do more?" When they got a little older and found bathroom words humorous, only my wife and I knew what they were talking about when they would say "do more" and giggle.

From your children's perspective, their sex organs are no different from their ears or toes, though toilet training may focus more attention on their sex organs than ever before. I discovered this, and also my failure to give our son Dave the proper name for his penis, when he asked his grandpa, "Papa, wanna see my waddle?" How David came up with "waddle," I don't know. But he had just discovered his penis and thought his grandpa might be interested in seeing it too. A matter-of-fact response helps convey to our children that it's okay to talk about our private parts as well as our ears and toes. In time they'll become sensitive and learn when and with whom they discuss these things.

Giving Independence

Related to the question of controlling the two-year-old is the question of independence. How do you give independence to children this age without having them go off the deep end?

Independence is important for children of all ages because it offers freedom to explore the unknown and to try out—their way—the untried. These freedoms are essential to the developmental process because much of children's development isn't *directive* but *reactive*. As they explore and try new things, children react to new and different circumstances, handling them in their own unique way. They learn by trial and error how workable their solution is.

For example, the weekend my wife and I took care of Jeremy and his sister, Heather, we took them to Virginia Beach. The surf was pretty rough and the undertow strong. I warned Jeremy several times not to get in too deep or he would get knocked down by a wave or the undertow.

Jeremy, being the enthusiastic, I-can-do-anything child that he is, wouldn't listen to me. I thought this would be a good opportunity to let natural consequences temper his lack of caution. The moment I let him run free, he charged for the surf, only to be slapped down by a wave and sucked toward the surf by the undertow.

Having purposely stood close by for the rescue, I calmly picked him up and delivered him to dry land, where he sputtered and coughed. The experience wasn't bad enough to make him afraid of the water, but it was jolting enough to make him respect it. I didn't have to warn him again the rest of the day. His reaction to the experience was caution and prudence.

Harold Wilke, a marvelous Christian born with no arms, tells of how his mother's tough parenting helped him grow in independence. Her willingness to let him struggle gave him the will and the courage to persevere through a difficult handicap. "I was 2 or 3 years old, sitting on the floor of my bedroom of our home, trying to get a shirt on over my head and around my shoulders, and having an extraordinarily difficult time. I was grunting and sweating, and my mother just stood there and watched. Obviously (looking back on this from hearing about it a long time later), I realized that her arms must have been held rigidly at her side, every instinct in her wanted to reach out and do it for me, as she kept those arms tight at her side. Finally, her neighbor, a woman friend, turned to her and said in exasperation, 'Ida, why don't you help that child?' My mother responded through gritted teeth, 'I *am* helping him.'"

We parents aren't smart enough to plan all life's experiences for our children. They need independence to explore the world and learn by doing.

Two-year-olds and teenagers offer a unique challenge, however. These are two major periods of breaking away from parental restraint and a time when they are very sensitive to being told no. Our children often believe they're ready to take on the world before they are adequately mature or prepared. This requires us to use three principles of granting independence.

1. *Say no only when it's necessary.* Reserve no only for those issues that may result in permanent damage. Sometimes parents will battle their children over unnecessary issues. For example, Kim insists that she doesn't want to eat. Is she not hungry or is she stubborn? In the interest of her eating nourishing food, you can go along with this as long as she waits for the next nourishing meal and doesn't eat junk food between meals. Hungry children will eat almost anything put before them. But we must have the resolve to make them wait for the next meal. They'll be hungry by then!

2. *Use natural consequences.* Hunger, pain, and rebuff by peers all are natural consequences for bad decisions that our children will experience if we get out of the way and let nature take its course. This is one of the principles used in Alcoholics Anonymous and AlAnon. We are warned not to be enablers, people who protect substance abusers from their bad decisions. If parents protect children from their bad decisions, natural consequences will not work.

3. *Recognize challenges to your authority.* Are our two-year-olds resisting us because they want to do things differently? Or are they testing the boundaries we have set to see if we really are in charge? Sometimes this is difficult to know, but it usually comes through in their *attitude*, which says, "I'm going to do this and do it my way. What's more, I'm not going to do *anything* I don't want to do, no matter how much you insist on it."

When we pick up this attitude, *that's* the issue we must address. We must put it in words the child understands. It may be as direct as, "Who's boss here—me or you?" When said firmly, but in good humor, children usually respond.

Place in the Family

Two-year-olds are affected by their place in the family. It influences both their outlook and development.

One factor we have no control over is our child's birth order. Is the child the first or second born? Is this a middle child or an only child? Closely related to birth order are questions such as, Is this child the only boy in a family of girls or the only girl in a family of boys? Is the child sickly, requiring special attention, or is the child healthy and contented, functioning well on a minimum of parental care?

The oldest child frequently feels dethroned by the second child and tries to maintain superiority over the intruder. The second child constantly challenges the position of the first child and attempts to find a niche by succeeding where the older child isn't successful. This explains why in many families the first and second child are different.

Middle children are in a precarious position. They don't have the rights of the older children or the privileges of the younger. They often are caught in a competitive struggle with the older and younger children and may feel that the others are ganging up on them.

But we parents must reckon not only with our children's place in the family constellation but also with *their reaction* to that place. This is complicated by our not knowing what their true feelings are!

My two oldest sons were born only ten-and-a-half months apart. In many ways, we felt as if we were raising twins. Yet the boys were very different from each other. The older one, Steve, was physically active and demanding. Our second son, Dave, was a quiet child who was content to play in his crib or playpen. He never was a demanding child, at any age.

Without our knowing it—or their knowing it—the boys trained me and my wife to respond differently to them. Steve needed our time and attention to direct his energies constructively. Dave could entertain himself and seemed content to do so. As the boys grew older, Steve was quite verbal about his wants and wishes. At Christmas he could produce a list of what he wanted. But Dave seemed content to get whatever we wanted to give him.

My wife and I didn't realize until the boys were grown that Dave felt he came up on the short end most of the time. And though we should have recognized it when it was happening, the practical demands of raising Steve and Dave and their two brothers, Pete and Jon, didn't leave a lot of time to encourage Dave to get in touch with what he wanted and to speak up. Indeed, we were glad that Dave didn't put the same demands on us that Steve did. But we didn't know what was happening!

As our children grow up, we parents will often lament that we didn't do things differently. Be careful not to castigate yourself. You have no control over birth order and how siblings react to each other. And many times we simply don't know what's going on inside our children. No amount of understanding or vigilance can change these things.

Understanding and Handling Aggression

Throwing toys and hitting playmates are frequent forms of aggression seen in two-year-olds. Remembering where they are in their development helps us respond constructively.

Remember that until age two, children have been able to be self-centered and develop self-confidence through their freedom to explore their world with few hindrances.

But now at age two, they are expected to become cooperative members of society. Cooperation is a new idea to them and is foreign to their usual way of operating.

High-energy children have a further liability. They tend to be physically strong and quick for their age and temperamentally driven to obliterate obstacles with aggression. Low-energy children tend to be sneakier and passively aggressive. They often are successful at baiting the more active child, who usually comes off as the offender in any dispute.

High-energy children need an opportunity to discharge that energy with vigorous, active play. If your children spend a great deal of time at a baby-sitter, be sure that they are getting plenty of fresh air and exercise. Tiredness resulting from play isn't the same as the tiredness that results from lack of sleep. Children who don't get enough sleep tend to be irritable, while those tired from play are more mellow and ready to sleep.

It's important, however, to give high-energy children time to wind down when playtime is over. They are like spirited racehorses who need a walk to cool off before they are expected to settle down.

Parents and caregivers also need to consider their own bias when dealing with aggressive, physically active children. Sometimes people who tend to be quiet have little tolerance for boisterous, energetic children. Though the children's behavior may not be bad, their energy and loudness is irritating, and caregivers may react accordingly.

Establish rules of behavior that your two-year-old will understand, and apply them calmly and firmly. Here are some examples: toys will not be thrown for any reason, especially at people; children will not be permitted to push, shove, or hit other people.

The rule about hitting is important. Children need to

know that hitting another child out of frustration or anger isn't the same as being spanked. This is why it's important that spanking be done in a cool, matter-of-fact manner. It demonstrates that the spirit and intent is entirely different from what the child does. What is more, children must learn that it isn't up to them to administer justice. This is the role of the parent or the adult caregiver.

Children who insist on hurting others with their aggression should be isolated from the group. They need to know that the only way they can be part of the group is to control their aggression and respect the needs of others. Because children are social creatures and want to be part of the group, isolation encourages them to give up their self-centered aggression in order to join in.

Parents and caregivers also need to be alert to aggression that results from unspoken conflicts and fears. Often children (and their parents) are difficult to get along with because they are already in a bad mood. Remember that two-year-olds, who have been self-centered and self-confident all their lives, now are attempting to be self-determined. This is how they prove that they are separate and distinct from their parents. They face the awesome task of learning how to pursue their needs in a way that respects the needs of others. The fire of self-determination ought not to be extinguished but rather regulated, protecting other people from harm.

The Shy Child

We often are so concerned about aggression in the two-year-old that we don't give enough attention to shyness. Shy children often are physically and temperamentally the opposite of aggressive, high-energy children. They aren't as driven as high-energy children and therefore tend to hold back and size up a situation to decide how they want to proceed. Shy children need time and space to proceed at their own pace.

We should be careful, however, that shy children don't manipulate us into doing for them what they should do for themselves. When they are in a strange, new setting, it's appropriate for us to break the ice by encouraging play with other children and to help them get acquainted with the caregiver. But we can't stay with them forever. We must leave them and say good-bye. Shy children often cry when their mom or dad leaves, but that's part of tough parenting—to expect them to cope with circumstances they may not like.

Summary

Our task with our two-year-olds is to help these self-determined children learn the limits of self-determination. Make the boundaries wide enough to give them plenty of room to grow and develop. But make the boundaries firm enough so the children clearly know their limits. And be ready to enforce those limits when challenged. Tough parenting must make clear to the child that the parents are in charge.

5

Just When We Think the Storm Is Over: Ages Three and Four

Age three is the time for a child's parents to recover from the terrible twos and prepare for the fearsome fours. At about the age of three, most children reach a stage of equilibrium. They are at peace with themselves and feel that they can cope with people and the demands of life.

Some important things have happened now to bring about this equilibrium. First, motor skills have developed to the point where children are less frustrated. Their body begins to cooperate with their efforts to make it do what they want.

Second, they become more proficient in their verbal skills. They can express their feelings better. They can say what's bothering them rather than act it out in hitting or by having a temper tantrum. Whereas once they would hit Jeff, they now more frequently say, "Jeff makes me mad. I don't want to play with him any more."

Third, they are getting used to the idea of being a

separate person from their mother. If she did a good job of giving them independence and reducing the number of times she said no, they have discovered that they can function as people in their own right without any threat to their survival. This doesn't mean that we ignored discipline. It means that our children gained a great deal of security knowing their limits and having those limits enforced consistently.

Consistency is an important element in our children's security. They can relax with the certainty *that some things are true all the time.* They don't waste time going over old ground, trying to figure out when something is forbidden and when it is not. Having settled that, they can spend time learning new things.

This doesn't mean that we never change rules. Sometimes new circumstances require a modification of rules. Our children must know, however, that it's their *parents'* prerogative to change the rules and that they have a good reason for changing them.

Sometimes a precocious four-year-old will say, "How come you get to change rules and I don't?" The obvious answer needs to be stated: Because moms and dads are smarter than four-year-olds, and *they* are responsible to decide what should and shouldn't be done in this family.

It's important that we not be timid about asserting our parental mandate. We, not our children, are responsible for the discipline, direction, and security of the family. When the time comes that our children are old enough, smart enough, and able to take care of their own needs in life, they'll be released from the parental mandate and will be accorded adult status.

Consolidating the Gains

Tough parenting during times of equilibrium takes dedication. Parents are tempted to take a breather from the conflict of terrible twos and let their children coast through age three. But we should be as determined to have our children master developmental skills at three as we were at age two. At no stage of development are our children excused from the job of growing up or are we excused from facilitating it. The parental mandate requires us to understand the developmental needs of three-year-olds and be as vigilant as ever in monitoring the forces at work on our children.

Times of equilibrium are important opportunities to consolidate the gains made by the child during the previous stage of disequilibrium. Work to help your children maintain the gains they have made in language development, cooperation, and innocence.

Language Development By the time they are three years old, children have a workable knowledge of the English language. This is an important time to correct poor language use. Parents hold their children back by talking baby-talk and permitting their children to do so. The child who wants "a dink of wa wa" may sound cute to parents, but the child's speech development is hindered unless parents encourage proper pronunciation.

This is also a time to stretch children's vocabulary by using words suitable for a three-year-old. For example, when they say that they feel bad, do they mean that they feel sick or sad? We help our children express themselves better when we take time to find out what they feel and give them appropriate words to express the feeling.

Be aware of speech impediments and correct them before the child reinforces them through use. A common one is the lisp, where s sounds are made with the tongue between the front teeth. The s sound is to be made with the front teeth touching and the tongue out of the way.

Their grammar, pronunciation, and vocabulary are only as good as that used by their parents. Are we helping our children learn good English by the way we use it?

Cooperation Look for opportunities to consolidate gains in cooperation from your children. Though abstract thinking won't come until about age six, three-year-olds can reason simple instances of cause and effect. They can understand that you are glad when they do what you want and you are unhappy when they don't. Because they want to please, you can explain the importance of their asking instead of going ahead and doing what they want without permission. You can explain that when they ask permission, it makes you feel good to know that they want to please you.

This doesn't mean that they always will get their way. For example, if they ask for a cookie before supper, you'll have to say no. But because they can reason a bit, they'll understand that you don't want them to spoil their supper. With their new ability to be more patient, they'll be more likely to accept the idea of a cookie for dessert. And if they don't, here's where tough parenting insists calmly and firmly that this is the way it's going to be, even if it makes them unhappy. If we maintain consistency in our expectations during times of equilibrium, we can prevent our children from regressing in their behavior and development.

Tough Parenting and Innocence We can't and shouldn't hold back the normal developmental process of children. Indeed, this is the meaning of Proverbs 22:6—to bring up a child in the way he should go. The "way he should go" refers to the human developmental process that I have been describing.

Although tough parenting permits our children to be exposed to the realities of life and expects them to cope with those realities, we must realize that it's possible to expose young children to these realities too soon. Some things are just too overwhelming for three- and four-year-olds to deal with.

I remember a mother, an antiwar activist, who sought counseling for her child who was having nightmares and had become very fearful. The child had dreams that everybody died in a terrible explosion or they were horribly burned. This mother believed that her child was the victim of a hawkish power establishment. But the child would have known nothing of the dangers of nuclear destruction if her mother hadn't carefully taught it to her and let her see television shows on the subject. Yes, our children need to be taught about their world. But let them learn at the appropriate time and season.

Innocence is an important quality in children. It protects them from exposure to ideas and circumstances they aren't mature enough to understand or handle emotionally. American culture has forgotten this in its determination to educate children about everything they need to know with no thought of age-appropriateness.

Sex education is a good example. Is it age-appropriate or even necessary to teach young children about AIDS and safe sex? Certainly if the subject comes up, that's another matter. For example, our children may hear of someone who is dying of AIDS and want to know what AIDS is. We can tell them that AIDS is a terrible disease people can die from and that they don't have to worry about getting it themselves. But at age three, children don't need to know that AIDS can be transmitted sexually and that they should use a condom when engaging in sex!

Television plays a major role in the loss of our children's innocence. Even on so-called "family" shows, young children can hear about subjects such as drug and alcohol use, marital infidelity, masturbation, safe sex, or breast augmentation. As parents, we should carefully screen programs before allowing children to view them.

I have no argument that some day our children should learn about these things. But in the normal developmental process, there is a proper time. Children who can't cognitively grasp the full meaning and implications of what they learn will fill in the details with their own imagination.

Dealing with the Special Needs of Three-Year-Olds

Because three- and four-year-olds are at different places in their development, each has special needs and parents have special concerns. Some of the special needs of three-year-olds include dealing with imaginary friends, modesty and sexuality, and gender development.

Imaginary Friends "Billy wants breakfast too," three-year-old Allison informs her mother as she holds out a piece of toast to her imaginary friend in the empty chair by the table. Her mother knows not to be alarmed. Imaginary friends are part of Allison's make-believe world, and they help her make a transition from the uncertainties of where she is socially to where she needs to go. Billy is a constant companion who always does what Allison wants and will take the blame for her mischief.

Not all children have imaginary friends. Some, through pretend play with other children, invent situations that they are able to play out with each other. It's a safe way to explore social situations that they may be fearful or uncertain about. For example, they may play cars and have accidents that send people to the hospital. By imagining the outcome with the help of their friends, they are able to get a feel for what they might do or how they might feel if this really were to happen.

Allison's imaginary friends do the same thing. They help her make her transition into socially new or unknown situations and help test existing rules. For example, she knows that when she is put to bed at night, the rule is that she stays there. However, she may appear in the living room where her mom and dad are watching television and inform them that Billy told her to do it. The parents can then say, "Tell Billy the rule is that you stay in bed when you're put there."

As Allison approaches age four, she'll become more interested in playing *with* other children, and her imaginary friends will disappear. She'll join other children in pretend play that will help her imagine how she would behave, and should behave, in various social situations.

Modesty and Sexuality At every age children cognitively learn new things and need to learn the proper social response. In a normal household, family members sometimes inadvertently find each other in various stages of undress. Parents who handle the episode in a matter-of-fact manner help children assimilate new information about modesty and privacy without being frightened that they have come across a new and dreaded experience that is to be avoided—nudity!

For example, when three-year-old Matt walks in a room where his mother is dressing, she can turn her back to him and say, "Matt, please go out and close the door. I'm getting dressed." Matt naturally is curious about his mommy's body. But his mom needs to let him know that her body is something private and that the socially appropriate thing is to respect that privacy.

Children who get a tongue-lashing for their natural curiosity may develop an inappropriate response to nudity. They may become extremely self-conscious about their own body and as adults may find it difficult to share themselves sexually with their spouse.

The other extreme is the family who, in the interest of letting the child find out about the body, actually encourages nudity. This is unwise.

Children must learn about personal boundaries. Our bodies are something private, and we are to respect the privacy of others. When we handle normal encounters with nudity in family life with a calm, modest response, our children learn by our behavior that our bodies are something private but nothing to be ashamed of.

Nudity between brothers and sisters should be handled the same way. One complication is that they'll be naturally curious about each other and want to observe the differences between the two of them. When parents come across this kind of natural exploration, it's important to avoid an emotionally charged response. In a matter-of-fact way the children should be told, "The penis [or vagina] is a very special part of you, so if you have a question, talk to either your dad or me instead of to other kids, okay?"

In answering questions about sex, it's important to remember that teaching small children is reactive rather than directive. We don't sit down with our four-year-old children at some appointed time and give them the birds-and-bees lecture, although age-appropriate books about the human body are good teaching tools. They learn about sex in bits and pieces as they grow up by the normal encounters they experience in family living. Sometimes parents tell their children too much at one time.

Another concern parents have is masturbation. Children, in the process of discovering their bodies, will find that they get pleasure out of manipulating their genitals. But don't assume that your young son has an erection because he's having an erotic experience. He probably has a full bladder. If he plays with his erection, ask him if he has to go to the bathroom. This usually takes care of the problem.

The little boy who continually pulls at himself may not be masturbating but may be experiencing discomfort because of a rash or tight-fitting clothes. He may also develop a habit of playing with himself, not because it's sexually stimulating, but simply because his penis is there. The habit, as all childish habits, should pass in time. Just don't make a big issue over it unless it persists over several months, and then seek your doctor's counsel.

Little girls eventually discover that pressing on the clitoris gives them pleasure. But this happens when they are a little older.

Gender Development With the rise of the women's liberation movement, efforts have been made to narrow the differences between males and females. Though I support a female's right to equal opportunities, equal treatment, and equal pay, I don't believe that females and males have the same physical and emotional makeup. Both need to develop a clear sense of their identity as a female or male. I especially see dangerous times ahead for boys and men who are floundering without a male identity.

Men today find it difficult to explain what it means to be a man, as distinct from a woman. To mask their missing sense of identity, some adopt a macho pose: tough, hard-drinking, profane, womanizing, and cynical. Others become quiet and inward and wait for the woman to make the first move in defining what her male partner is to be like. Then the man attempts to fill that role.

How is it possible, in a cultural atmosphere like this, to help boys and girls develop a sense of uniqueness about their roles as male or female? Our difficulty is compounded by the high percentage of educators and mental-health professionals who believe that the difference between the genders is minimal and that any apparent differences are imposed by society.

In 1974, psychologists Eleanor Maccoby and Carol Jacklin wrote an excellent book, *The Psychology of Sex Differences*. Though their careful research and objective conclusions received little notice, their findings are extremely enlightening. For instance, they found that young boys tend to engage in rough-and-tumble play more frequently than girls.[1] Boys base their choice of playmates largely on the other person's game skills. Girls, on the other hand, tend to play more quietly with people they like.[2] While boys tend to play in larger groups or "gangs," girls focus their play on one or two best friends or "chumships," the psychologists found.[3]

Further, they discovered that as girls get older, they establish distance or closeness with each other based on how well they know the other person. This is less true for boys. Two boys will more readily accept a third into the group than two girls will.[4] And girls are more likely to tell each other secrets and be self-disclosing than boys.[5]

While it's true that much sex-typed behavior is learned, the readiness to learn has a *biological basis*. And I believe an essential difference between boys and girls is the biological basis of boys' aggressiveness.

Your baby-sitter or day-care provider may not share this view and may be very intolerant of your four-year-old son's aggressiveness. Be alert to attitudes that differ from yours. Be prepared to correct your baby-sitter's perspective or be ready to find another baby-sitter. One of your first clues of a caregiver's intolerance is complaints that your son is always "in trouble." Spend a little time observing how your son's caregivers handle him.

I'm not suggesting that we excuse bad behavior or allow boys to victimize other children. But caregivers need extra patience in handling active boys.

An Important Difference Between Ages Three and Four

Age three is a stage of equilibrium; age four returns to disequilibrium. It doesn't happen suddenly, but sometime around age three-and-a-half, our children begin to be a little less secure about themselves, their surroundings, and their relationships to other people. A major reason for this is the further development of cognitive and social skills.

Younger children study older children to get some clue as to what's ahead for them and how to handle the new, uncertain future. The typical four-year-olds our children watch are loud, demanding children who behave much like big, savvy two-year-olds.

Given this reality, we must closely monitor our children's development as they move from age three to age four. At age three, our children tend to engage in parallel play. They'll play side by side, but much of it is by themselves rather than with each other. Four-year-olds tend to engage in play with each other. A major step in social development in our children's growth from age three to age four is their learning to be *part* of a peer group.

With a four-year-old, we should be prepared for another problem that we don't have with a three-year-old. When children start playing together, they learn what other parents allow their children to do, and they may challenge our rules and expectations. For example, when we tell them they can't do something, we should be prepared for an angry, "Why can't I do it? My friends can."

The answer is, "I know this doesn't seem fair to you, but I'm saying no because I care about you, and I want what is best. Even though your friends may do it, we don't think any four-year-old should."

Tough parenting must win the day. Be prepared to have your reasons invalidated, but don't argue their validity.

Just walk away from further arguments. Four-year-olds really don't want to know why. They just want their way.

Monitoring the influence of our children's four-year-old friends is a big job. But we *must*, at this point in our child's life, begin to exercise control that continues until the child leaves home as a young adult. Tough parenting requires us to control our children's relationships, having absolute veto power over their friendships. When we begin doing this as early as ages three and four and apply the rule consistently, we should have little difficulty enforcing the rule when our children are in their teens.

Dealing with the Special Needs of Four-Year-Olds

Though we may not be able to anticipate every problem with our four-year-olds, knowing where they are in their development and why they behave as they do can help us deal effectively with the problems that arise. Age four is a time of disequilibrium. No longer satisfied with the gains enjoyed at age three, four-year-olds are out to conquer new territory. Remember that disequilibrium is a time of growth. Times of equilibrium with our children tend to make us forget that disequilibrium is coming again. And when it comes, we sometimes feel that something is wrong with our children because they no longer are the genial, cooperative, nice people they used to be.

Parents often say that their children are going through a stage. And indeed, they are. But given time, this too will pass, and everyone will enjoy the respite of equilibrium again.

The Positive Side of Friendships Though friends can have a negative influence on four-year-olds, friends are important to our children's proper social development. We live in a society with certain rules and conventions, and our children learn how to make their way in society through interaction with their friends. They learn to express themselves as their peers do. They learn to give and get information in ways that are normal for their peer group. When their style of communication and their behavior is appropriate for their peer group, they are most likely to be accepted by them.

When children have disputes with their friends, we shouldn't interfere. Certainly we should keep them from hurting each other. But disputes give our children an opportunity to learn to negotiate their differences. Remember that tough parenting doesn't protect children from adversity. We should be ready to keep them from being overwhelmed. But children are social creatures, and they learn to develop social skills by trial and error. We can give them basic information about what's appropriate, but they must develop the skills by interacting with peers.

Though it's important that we monitor friendships, it's extremely important to give our children an opportunity to develop behavior appropriate to their peer group. If we keep our children from peer-group interaction, we may arrest their social development. We all have seen children who, though intelligent and morally circumspect, are misfits in society because they never developed behavior and language appropriate to their peer group.

The early development of social skills is important because once children get behind and begin to feel like misfits, they tend to withdraw and fail to master social skills at each stage of development. Christian parents must realize that we are responsible to raise children who aren't just intelligent and God-fearing. We are responsible to see that they are able to function in society. Jesus Christ was God, but his divinity didn't obscure his humanity. He was a winsome, dynamic person, who was constantly sought out by others.

We can monitor our children's friendships and activities by doing two things. First, we should know something about the parents of our children's close friends. We may not know them personally, but we should know enough about them to be confident they have parenting principles and objectives that are similar to ours. If we don't know enough about the parents, we can call them and invite them over for coffee. We can simply say that their child has become our child's close friend, and we would like to get acquainted.

The response you get will tell you something about their parenting style. They should want to know you too, because your child is an influence on their child. And if they give their child permission to go places with you without knowing anything about you, they may not be bad parents, but they are careless. You don't have to become close friends with every parent, but you should have enough contact to know what kind of parents they are.

Second, we can invite our child's friends to take part in our family activities. We quickly learn the kind of influence the friends have on our child. We also have an opportunity to guide the friendship and give direction to it.

Embarrassing Remarks and Immodesty Though friendships are important to four-year-olds, friends tend to encourage inappropriate language and behavior. The language skill of four-year-olds is developed to the point where they can plunge ahead in their exploration of the world around them. But they lack the social skills to know how to do it appropriately.

Four-year-olds love to ask why. Sometimes they do it because they are truly curious, other times because they like to be silly. Sometimes their whys can be a cause of embarrassment. We can't always be sure whether they don't know any better (lack of social skill) or if they're trying to get a reaction out of us.

For example, you are having coffee with a friend when your four-year-old daughter pipes up, "Mommy, why does that lady have a mustache?" Most people realize that four-year-olds are socially inexperienced and will help ease the embarrassment. Or you might say, "I can see my daughter needs some help in developing her social skills," and let it go at that. If your daughter doesn't pick up from your reaction that she has said something inappropriate and continues, you may need to say, "Honey, come here a minute with me." Take her to another room and quietly explain to her that people's feelings can be hurt when we point out things that look different about them. This usually is sufficient when it's merely a social blunder.

Children also stare at people who are disfigured. They need to know that we understand that they've never seen anything like that before, but staring may make people feel sad because they're different.

Sometimes four-year-olds have fun with language by deliberately using bathroom words. If they say something inappropriate, a simple reprimand will do: "It's not polite to talk that way. I don't want to hear that again." If they continue, the issue is no longer the bathroom words but their challenge to your authority. In this case, time out—having your child spend some time alone in a room until he or she is in better control—is in order.

Immodesty can be handled the same way. Four-year-olds often find the shock value of immodesty amusing—like running through the room naked while you're having coffee with your friend. Again, an immediate, private conversation about the inappropriateness of the behavior should be enough. If it isn't, then time out may be necessary.

Conscience The development of conscience and moral reasoning takes a lifetime. As with other human qualities, conscience needs to be cultivated at each stage of development. This cultivation comes in the form of information and social interaction that helps a child learn what is considered good and bad.

We get our notions of good and bad from the character of God. Whatever is true of God is good. Whatever is untrue of him or foreign to him is bad. For example, the Bible says that God is light and in him is no darkness at all. Darkness, subterfuge, and lies are, therefore, unacceptable.

All people know this because God has revealed himself in nature (Ps. 19:1–2). Not only that, people are created with a conscience (John 1:9). Their conscience lets them know when they are obeying or disobeying God. Humanity's problem with disobedience isn't that people don't know any better. Their problem is that they know and they rebel against that knowledge and pervert it (Rom. 1:18–23).

We who have become members of God's family through faith in Jesus Christ are much like children in a human family. Because God is a person, family harmony (the religious word is "fellowship") requires that our behavior as God's children be consistent with the nature of our Father. When it's not (we call it sin), we are out of fellowship with our Father. He can't go along with our behaving in a manner that is foreign to him and to what he wants in his children.

The way back to fellowship is to confess sin (1 John 1:9). The word *confess* in the Bible literally means "to say the same thing as." When we say the same thing about our behavior that the Father does, we are in *agreement*. Agreement is the foundation of fellowship and harmony, whether it's in God's family or the human family.

The father and mother in a human family have moral character, though not perfect, like God's. They want to instill that moral character in their children. They give their children information about what is expected of them, and in social intercourse with the child, they monitor the child's behavior on a daily basis, correcting the child when he or she does wrong, and chastising the willfully disobedient child, just as God chastises us.

The conscience and moral development of the child is a very practical matter. It enables the family to live in *harmony*. We are able to live in fellowship with each other *because we agree with each other*.

This doesn't mean that our children must dot every *i* and cross every *t* as we do. There is room both in the church and in the Christian family for differences. We aren't clones. But just as God keeps differences in the church within acceptable limits, parents keep their children's differences within certain limits.

When four-year-old Sherry lies to her parents, though she may not be able to understand that lying is a sin against a holy God, she can understand that lying hurts the harmonious relationship she has with her mom and dad. She and her parents no longer agree on what the truth is about the matter. And the only way parent and child can regain that harmony is for the child to admit that she is wrong and agree with her parents on the truth of the matter.

As our children go through this process over their lifetime, they begin to discover that good conscience and moral reasoning not only make for a harmonious family life but also have practical benefits in relationships with others. They discover that trustworthiness encourages others to trust them.

Dealing with dishonesty or any other moral lapse in a four-year-old needs to be dealt with gently, however.

Angry accusations such as, "You're lying to me!" are inappropriate. It's far better to say, "Honey, I'm having trouble believing what you're saying. And when you keep telling me that you're right, it makes me feel sad. It makes me not want to trust you."

Though we ought not to be harsh and rejecting, our children will experience a breach in their relationship to us. And because our children value that relationship above all other relationships, given time, they'll come to terms with what they are doing so they can feel close again to their parents.

This assumes that we parents create a loving, accepting, harmonious atmosphere that makes our children glad to be members of the family. And when they do confess their wrong, they need to feel our acceptance.

Preschool At age four, many children are involved in preschool activities. Preschool may or may not be advisable for your four-year-old, particularly if your child isn't ready for structured classroom work.

Children need opportunity for unstructured play, which gives them opportunity to develop physically, emotionally, and socially at a rate they feel comfortable with. When they are put in preschool too soon, some children miss out on the opportunity for the amount of unstructured play they need. What is designed to aid in their development actually hinders it because the programmed nature of preschool may not allow enough freedom for children to develop at their own rate and in their own unique way.

When children are exposed too soon to "academic" exercises, they sometimes experience burnout and an aversion to study when they start school. Some children aren't ready to begin structured classroom work until they are six years old. Nothing is wrong with their mental, physical, emotional, or social competency. It's just that children develop at different rates.

Children who develop later often are labeled as bad or disruptive. And the pity of it is they aren't bad. If they are disruptive, it's probably because they were put into a program not suited for them. Parents and teachers need to give the child more time to develop the interest needed to participate in programmed learning. It's not just a matter of attention span. It's a matter of getting out of their own world and into the larger world beyond them.

Consider these factors in determining whether or not to put your four-year-old in preschool or day care.

1. *Interest level.* Are your children able to show interest in activities that are suggested by others, or are they interested only in play and activities they suggest?

2. *Attention span.* Are your children able to show sustained involvement in a scheduled activity, such as sitting with a parent and reading a book? Or are they easily distracted, moving from one activity to another as the mood strikes them?

3. *Openness.* At the other extreme, do your children limit themselves to a few activities and act uneasy about trying new things?

4. *Awareness level.* Are your children so compliant that they never are mischievous and don't have the kind of curiosity about things that other children do?

5. *Physical readiness.* Do your children eat and sleep well and have bladder and bowel control with the exception of occasional nighttime bed wetting?

6. *Emotional readiness*. Emotionally, are your children able to be spontaneous in affection to those close to them and able to accept adult authority without being overly compliant or uncooperative?

7. *Relational maturity*. Do your children have the ability to make and maintain peer relationships, including the ability to settle their own disputes?

As a parent, you know your child better than anyone else does. As you look at this list and consider other factors not listed, trust your intuition in making your decision about preschool. And don't hesitate to delay preschool for your child. It's far better to start a child a little later than too early.

Summary

It's hard not to relax and let our children do as they wish when they're cooperative three-year-olds. Yet tough parenting requires us to protect our children from unwholesome experiences.

We want to be sure that they have good male and female role models as they develop their gender identity. And their innocence needs to be preserved, even if monitoring their television watching is an extra burden to us.

The people they see as role models in real life and on television have a profound effect on their idea of what it means to be a male or a female. Saying no to shows they want to see may bring tears, but it's better to have tearful three-year-olds than kids who develop a warped view of life because they are exposed to too much too soon.

The most trying task with four-year-olds will be monitoring their friendships. But accept it as a major task of tough parenting. If you start out right, insisting on your power to veto friendships, you'll find it easier to do when they get older. And they'll be more accepting of the idea.

With our one- and two-year-olds we spent a great deal of time protecting them from themselves. Three- and four-year-olds need tough parents to protect them from unwholesome influences in their new and larger world.

6

Capitalizing on Cooperation:
Age Five

Age five is not just a stage of equilibrium; it's also a milestone. Children who started life as totally self-centered people have by age five learned to care about other people's needs and feelings and are cooperative and ready to learn. By now they have discovered, or are on the brink of discovering, that the way *they* think things should be isn't necessarily the only way, and they're willing to listen to parents and teachers.

Tough parenting may be difficult with five-year-olds. It's tough for parents because it's difficult to say no to children who are trying to please them. It's tough for five-year-olds because they don't understand why their parents say no. But if our children trust us, they'll be able to defer to us, even though they don't like to be told no. This dynamic prepares the way for them later to accept that God is loving and good, even though he may say no to some of their requests.

Preschool and kindergarten are designed to help our children learn structure and classroom procedure. Though our five-year-olds should be ready to handle preschool or kindergarten, they may not be ready for structured classroom study until they're six years old. Some parents, afraid that others will think their child is slow, sometimes start their children in school too soon.

Age five is a time to strengthen what our children have achieved. We should look at three areas of development to determine if our children have accomplished what is normally expected of a five-year-old: physical and intellectual development, social development, and psycho-sexual development.

Physical and Intellectual Development

Pediatricians tell us that five-year-olds should be able to stand and hop on one foot and show skill in rolling, sliding, and swinging. They should be able to match ten to twelve colors, copy letters, and draw a human body with a head and facial features filled in. They enjoy reciting rhymes, telling stories, and having books read to them. They ask the meaning of abstract words. They build complex structures out of play materials and are dramatic and imaginative in play. They enjoy companionship and understand the need for rules and fair play. They have an understanding of time and are generally sensible, restrained, and independent.[1]

The Importance of Books Books are a primary source of our children's learning throughout their lives. We can encourage our children to read by reading ourselves and by reading age-appropriate books to them. We should encourage our children to know the titles of their books and what they're about.

Children should have their own books and their own "library." Don't throw their books in the toy box with the toys. Show that books are special by having a separate shelf for them.

When our children start school, they probably will have enough reading drills without needing to do more at home. Make reading at home fun for them. If they initiate the activity, let them point out words they know or let them read to you if they're advanced enough to do that. But don't pressure them. Remember, make books fun.

We also might share with them what we're reading in the newspaper or news magazines, particularly if pictures accompany the story. We tend to think our children are indifferent to what's going on in the world. But they're curious, particularly if a picture and story describe something they hear adults talking about. We can do the same with television news stories. The special attention given to children by Mr. Rogers and Peter Jennings during the 1991 war with Iraq illustrates my point.

Video Games and Computers Children of the nineties enjoy a new adjunct to learning—video games and computers. Used constructively, both tools can be a boon to learning. Children can practice mathematical and verbal skills, create visual designs, play baseball, and fight monsters. Not only do the games offer intellectual stimulation, they also help develop eye-hand coordination.

Because many of the games use a combat or competition motif, boys tend to find them more interesting than girls do. If your daughter shows interest in the computer or video games, take her to a video game store and let her select something appropriate to her interests.

Video games and computers have their downside, however. Our children may isolate themselves from social contact with others because video games and computers offer the opportunity for solitary play. As with everything, we need to insist on balance.

Another parental objection is the violent nature of many video games. Some are war games that involve planes, ships, and tanks. Others involve combat between people. The argument is that we teach our children to be violent by example, an objection also raised over violence on television.

I believe that children are able to distinguish between the fantasy of video-game violence and the real thing. Before video games and television, kids played cowboys and Indians, cops and robbers, and other "violent" games, like zooming with toy cars and having them crash. Fantasy is an important part of our children's development. Of more concern to me than violent themes is that video games provide a ready-made fantasy. I wonder how much creativity they lose by not needing to imagine their own fantasy worlds.

The "Hyper" Child By the time children are five years old, we begin to have concerns about the "hyperactive" child. I put the word in quotation marks because much of what is labeled as hyperactivity isn't hyperactivity at all; often it's just overactivity, a five-year-old's inability to sit still. Truly hyperactive children are more than overactive: their activity is haphazard and poorly organized. If you have questions about your child, see a child psychologist. The opinions of teachers, friends, and other parents aren't sufficient.

Psychologists find that about three percent of the school-age population fits the diagnostic criteria of hyper-activity, and many of those children have attention deficit disorder (ADD). The fact that this disorder is *ten times* more common in boys than in girls suggests that something unique to the male gender makes boys more vulnerable. This fact may bias elementary-school teachers, prompting them to mislabel overactive boys as hyperactive.

What can you do if a child psychologist determines your child is hyperactive? First, you can provide a home environment that counterbalances hyperactivity and ADD. Studies show that children living in a disorganized, chaotic environment where their developmental needs are neglected will have difficulty sustaining attention and engaging in goal-directed behavior. Try to keep your home life organized and stable, providing a calming effect on your child. Cut down the amount of noise your child encounters. Turn off radios and televisions that are on as background sound. Minimize the use of noisy appliances (vacuum cleaners, fans, electric tools) when the child is around. Keep the child from places where lots of movement of people or objects will be an underlying distraction.

Use drug therapy as a last resort. Evidence shows that drug doses high enough to control hyperactivity not only inhibit the child's ability to learn but also produce other harmful side effects.

Social Development

We should examine at least two areas of social development in our five-year-olds: affection and communication. How do they show affection and communicate with siblings, friends, caregivers, and most important, their own parents? How they demonstrate these social skills with us depends a lot on *how we demonstrate these social skills with them!*

Affection Some children will show their affection spontaneously. They will hug and kiss parents and grandparents with no self-consciousness at all. Their words and tone of voice with friends and siblings will sound caring, and they feel comfortable with touching.

Other children tend to be more aloof. The nonverbal message they convey is, "Give me space." Most people are unaware of nonverbal messages like this, though we give and receive them every day. And though we respect those messages, we usually don't ask that they be put into words or ask why the message is given. As a result, our earliest social behaviors are reinforced without our being aware of it.

Many times the reinforcing of cold, aloof behavior begins as early as infancy. Babies who are squirmy and rigid and who sometimes cry when we try to cuddle them, train us to leave them alone. And when we leave them alone, we teach them to expect us to leave them alone because this has been their experience for as long as they can remember.

Sadly, they don't know they're making people believe that they want to be left alone. That's why it's imperative that part of our child's socialization include talks about nonverbal behavior and what the behavior means.

Children tend to deny the existence of nonverbal behavior. And this denial is fundamental to manipulation. By sending nonverbal messages, they are able to demand what they want without taking responsibility for asking for it. When we permit this behavior, we teach them to be manipulators. Don't do it!

If your children are cool, aloof, withdrawn, or not affectionate, describe the behavior and ask them if they prefer to be left alone. They must accept the responsibility for distance and understand that it's what *they* do, not what others do, that results in social isolation.

Some children simply are less demonstrative than others. They may show their affection in the thoughtful things they do rather than by kisses and hugs. If your children are like this, reinforce their behavior by recognizing it for what it is. And help them understand that this is their style of showing affection. When they begin to date and eventually marry, it needs to be clear to them and to their spouse what their style of affection is. When this isn't clear, they may be hurt because someone they love doesn't respond to their affection.

Fathers must be careful that they don't discourage their sons from showing affection with kisses and hugs. By kissing and hugging their little boys, dads send the message that it's okay for males to do this.

Communication The tone of voice our children use with us tells us a lot about their attitudes and feelings. If our children are to be honest and not manipulative, we must talk about their negative tone of voice or the angry expression on their face. But what about *our* tone of voice and angry expression? What do these convey to our children? They often convey that we find something wrong with *them*.

My wife, Fay, grew up feeling like this. As a youngster, she was taller than the other girls her age in school, so she knew she was different. But her mother, responsible for buying her clothes, put the icing on the cake. Many times out of frustration she would say things like, "You big ox. Why can't you wear clothes off the rack like other kids?"

I was dumbfounded when I learned this after many years of marriage. When I met Fay, I was instantly struck by her beauty. She had the stature and bearing of a model. But in her mind, on the authority of her mother, she was a big ox.

When we are displeased with our children, we should direct our remarks at their *behavior*, not their person. They can change their behavior. But even children know they can't change their temperament and personality, particularly when they bear the family curse of being "just like" a much-ridiculed or maligned parent or grandparent. And when we see behavior change, we should reinforce it by letting them know we notice the change and that we like it.

For example, we can say, "Laurie, I appreciate your picking up your dirty clothes and putting them in the hamper. This is something I have fussed about, and I appreciate your listening to my feelings about it."

There's nothing wrong with encouraging our children to do things because it pleases us. This is essential to family life. We show we care by respecting the needs and feelings of those we love, a dynamic our children will carry over into their relationships.

Our children learn by trial and error. Not only do they need to know when they're doing it right, they need to know we appreciate the change for the better. The testy parent who says, "That's the way you ought to do it all the time," sends the child a very disheartening message. The message is, "Don't think that pleasing me is going to make our relationship happy and harmonious." Our children need to know that pleasing parents and other people *does* make for better relationships.

Tips on Talking with Kids

As you talk with your children, keep the following in mind:

1. *Listen for the feelings behind the words.* Ken's sister receives a very expensive doll for her birthday, but Ken calls it stupid and ridicules his sister when she plays with it. He's obviously unhappy about it. You can say, "Ken, when I hear you call your sister's doll stupid, I wonder if you feel bad because she seems to get nicer things than you get."

Ken may not be able to answer immediately, or he may deny that's how he feels. Trust your parental intuition, and if you think that's how he really feels, put your arm around him and tell him, "It's okay to say you feel that way, if that's how you really feel."

This does two things for Ken. First, it puts him in touch with the real issue. Second, he learns that it's okay to say how he really feels. When children find that the constructive expression of their feelings helps people to understand and care about them, they're likely to grow up as good communicators.

2. *Listen to and help interpret your child's generalities.* Sherry comes in crying. She has been playing with her friends and can't seem to master the art of catching a softball. Her friends contribute to her bad feelings by calling her clumsy. Sherry wails, "I can't do anything right."

There's a big difference between lacking eye-hand coordination and not doing anything right. But be careful you don't dismiss her feelings by pointing that out to her immediately. You could say, "I heard the kids call you clumsy, Sherry. They said they didn't want you on their team. That really must have hurt your feelings."

When Sherry is convinced that you understand how she feels and why, she's ready to hear that she does do some things right and better than the other kids. She may not be gifted at physical things, but she may have artistic or musical talent that is superior for her age. And she may need to associate with kids who value, and whose parents value, something other than accomplishment in physical things.

Compensation is a major way our children cope. Tough parenting realizes that trial and error teaches our children what they're good at and what they're not good at. And tough parenting helps children accept that reality. This opens the door to new possibilities for our children and encourages them to channel their interest and energies in that direction.

Psycho-sexual Development

By age five, our children arrive at a milestone in psycho-sexual development. Two of the more important issues that are usually settled by age five are gender identity and the Oedipus complex—sometimes called "family romance."

Gender Identity Human sexuality involves not only anatomy—the physical differences between the sexes—but also a sense of what it means to be male or female. This includes a psychological predisposition or interest in sexual contact and, in later years, the ability to perform sexually.

Parents look for evidences that their child has a strong sense of gender identity and, in accord with that gender identity, heterosexual interest. Science hasn't yet made it possible to guarantee parents that their children will not be homosexual or transsexual (desiring to be the opposite gender). Though much has been written about homosexuality, the experts can't agree on what makes a person homosexual. How much is nature gone awry and how much is improper nurture still is a matter of debate.

Maccoby and Jacklin, in their book *The Psychology of Sex Differences*, offer some helpful information about psychological sex differentiation. They suggest that gender identity is influenced by genetic makeup, imitation, and parental anxiety.

1. Genetic makeup. Our children's genetic makeup greatly influences their *readiness* to learn a particular kind of behavior, whether labeled male or female. For example, boys are more ready to learn aggressive behavior than girls are because of their male biology. Though the behavior is learned, there is a greater *readiness* to learn it.[2]

This raises some important questions psychologists have yet to answer. What happens when this genetic readiness is absent? Do the children just find it more difficult to learn the behaviors associated with their gender? Or do they learn them but never really feel comfortable with them? Lacking this genetic readiness, do they later adopt a sexual orientation they feel more comfortable with? Our children's genetic makeup plays a larger part in their psychosexual development than was once thought.

2. *Imitation.* A second finding, which requires more study, is that children do not simply imitate the behaviors of same-sex people. How children *process* the information they observe is all-important. Children commonly *distort* what they see and hear and come up with conclusions that are contrary to reality.

An example is given of a four-year-old girl who insisted that females could be nurses, but only males could be doctors. This conclusion wasn't based on imitation of the most readily available model, her mother—who was a doctor! The girl had arrived at her conclusion based on stereotypes she had seen on television, in movies, in books, and in her limited life experience.

As with most childlike conclusions, her mother's exception to the rule was ignored. But what did she think of her *mother's* gender identity? Did her mother qualify as a full-fledged female? Was her femaleness discounted because she was a doctor? Was her mother not to be a model for her at all because she violated the rule that only males can be doctors?

We can't begin to imagine a three-, four-, or five-year-old's fantasies about gender identity and sexuality. Indeed, it's surprising to me that so many of us turn out to be as well adjusted sexually as we are!

The problem is complicated by the fact that three- and four-year-olds don't always know that their gender is permanent. And they aren't always certain who is male and who is female, an important consideration given the fact that gender identity is to a large degree imitative. Though we may be sensitive about sex-stereotyping, we should be careful to provide adequate male and female models for our children.

3. *Parental anxiety*. How parents respond to a child's psycho-sexual development also influences the child's gender identity. Parents often worry more about their sons than their daughters, perhaps because male homosexuality is more prevalent and open than female homosexuality. In this setting the boy is more likely than the girl to be chided for inappropriate gender behavior. He's likely to be told it's sissy behavior to put on lipstick, while his sister's tomboy behavior may get no notice at all.

Does the greater incidence of homosexuality have anything to do with parents' greater anxiety about their son's gender identity than their daughter's? We don't have a reliable answer to that. But common sense should tell us that parental anxiety, for any reason, has a toxic influence on the home environment. Parents need to reinforce gender-typical behavior in their children and not react strongly to what is atypical. Our children's peers will help discourage atypical behavior.

The Oedipus Complex The Oedipus complex, a concept advanced by psychologist Sigmund Freud, involves a child's romantic love for the opposite-sex parent. In his book *How to Father*, Dr. Fitzhugh Dodson prefers to call it the "family romance" because all children go through the experience, and it shouldn't be considered abnormal.[3]

According to Dodson, little boys and girls experience the phenomenon differently. Boys, around age three, develop romantic feelings toward their mother. A boy may see his father as a rival and imagine that his father feels the same animosity toward him that he feels toward his father. Much of a boy's negative behavior toward his father rises out of these feelings of rivalry. He doesn't want his father to do anything for him. Only mother will do, whether it's to read him a story or listen to his complaints.

The father who is aware of what's going on will be careful not to demean, patronize, or tease his son. It's serious to the boy. Likewise, dads need to be aware that negative words and actions toward their son may be *interpreted* by the boy as evidences that the rivalry does indeed exist. Though they may be cautious about not leaving this impression, dads will find they aren't always successful. A father's patience and caring behavior toward the boy will do more than attempts to talk with him about what's happening. The child isn't mature enough to understand what's going on.

By age six, this should pass. The boy will realize that he can't marry his mom and take his dad's place. He will begin to identify with his father and will desire to be like him.

Girls face a similar problem with the family romance, but with a couple of complications. For as long as she can remember, a girl has had her need for love and affection fulfilled primarily by her mother. Now she feels rivalry with her mother yet still needs that affection. It's important for mothers to recognize this conflict, which will express itself in paradoxical behavior: on the one hand her daughter will be testy and push her away, and on the other, her daughter will want her affection and attention.

Or her daughter may be confused and tentative about her relationship with her mother.

The girl may not be very verbal about her feelings for her daddy because she still needs her mom. But she needs to know that her mom loves her and that she will not be ridiculed or rejected because she wants to take her mom's place.

Parents who have a healthy relationship and are obviously affectionate with each other help their children face the reality that no one is going to break them up. Parents also need to work together on their child's discipline and be careful that the child doesn't attempt to divide them on how to discipline. This only reinforces the child's fantasy that the same-sex parent can be displaced.

The developmental characteristics of the five-year-old described in this chapter may arrive later in some children, so we should be careful that we don't assume something is wrong with our five-year-olds if they don't fit the description. And above all, remember that when I talk about equilibrium and children being at peace with themselves and their world, I'm talking about something that's relative. Some children are easier to deal with during equilibrium. Others are just less difficult!

7

The Mystery Years—
What Is This Child Thinking?
Ages Six Through Ten

Ages six through ten, sometimes called middle childhood, is a stage of uncommunicativeness, a stage in which
our children become a mystery to us. Our kids are
uncommunicative because their interests are moving from
family to peer group. Concerned with fitting in, they spend
a lot more time working at their relationships to their
friends than to their family, and they want to be able to do
it without adult interference.

Sometimes our children are *deliberately* uncommunicative. We'll ask, "Where are you going?"

Our child answers, "Out."

"What are you going to do?"

"Nothing."

Our children are moving their interest from the family
to the peer group because they are trying to establish their
identity.

The Importance of Identity

The biggest concern our children have is their identity. Do other kids see them as leaders of the pack, or, if not leaders, supporters and members of the pack?

Children sometimes are unable to find identity with the group in socially acceptable ways, and they resort to socially unacceptable behavior. This behavior may get them excluded from the group, forcing them to establish their identity *apart* from the group.

I'm not talking about a loner. There's nothing wrong with a child being a loner, so long as he or she is content with that identity. The loners we have problems with are kids who don't want to be outside the group but who don't know how to become part of the group in socially acceptable ways. This was Doug's problem.

Doug's Struggle for Identity At age six, Doug had serious feelings of inferiority about his physical abilities and his small build. He always had been a sickly child and had heard from his parents as long as he could remember, "You can't do that—you'll have an asthma attack," despite the fact that Doug's doctor had never discouraged vigorous physical activity. As a result of his parents' fears, Doug never developed eye-hand coordination or the stamina to play kickball, catch, or games that other children could play.

Doug decided the best way to handle his feelings of physical inferiority was to accept the identity of weakling and simply not try anything that called for physical skill. He actually *worked* at establishing that identity. He usually could get out of having to participate in team sports at school by raising the fear of an asthma attack. His parents, teachers, and friends accepted and reinforced this.

Doug became dissatisfied with his underdog identity at age seven. Because so much of his early childhood was spent with books, he excelled at reading in school and was able to compensate for his lack of physical skill with academic achievement. This would have been a good solution, except that he didn't just compensate. He overcompensated. He looked for opportunities to parade before peers, teachers, and parents his superior academic ability.

By age ten he had completely alienated his peers with arrogant, snobbish behavior that said, "I'm better than the rest of you." And when the other kids excluded him from the group, that was okay with him. He was superior to them anyway. Though Doug's behavior socially alienated him, he had at least achieved his identity!

If Doug had been more like Jason, there would have been no problem. Jason also excelled in school. He too brought home papers and projects with A's on them. But Jason behaved differently from Doug. When Jason showed his accomplishments to his parents and they responded approvingly, Jason went on to other things, like playing with his friends or watching television. Jason knew that his parents were happy with his performance in school. He didn't need to solicit long and detailed praise to assure himself of that fact because he felt he had achieved his identity as a good student.

Attention-Getting Behavior Children who are unable to achieve their identity in socially acceptable ways most commonly resort to attention-getting behavior—any behavior intentionally designed to gain people's attention. But this kind of behavior is maladaptive and excessive, as the contrast between Doug and Jason illustrates.

Active children who resort to attention-getting behavior may try out the role of clown, bully, boss, or mother-superior. Passive children often try out less visible roles such as poor soul, immovable object, or helpless victim.

Doug tried out two roles. The first was weakling, which he used to relieve himself of the embarrassment of inept athletic skills. He then changed his underdog status to a second role, super intellect. Though the other kids didn't like his arrogant behavior, he didn't think anything was wrong with it; the other kids were just jealous of his superior performance. But in both cases, his behavior was extreme and designed to get attention.

When attention-getting behavior involves positive things like academic achievement, parents sometimes have difficulty seeing it as an identity problem. This is why Doug didn't get professional help until he was age ten. His parents didn't think he had an identity problem. But when he consistently alienated his peers, they realized he needed help.

Children who engage in attention-getting behavior often feel that they'll be loved only if they succeed. This is the conclusion I came to as a child. My father paid attention to me only when I had achieved something or had an opportunity to do so. I believe that much of my narcissistic behavior as a young adult, my need for approval and shame over failure, was the direct result of feeling that my father wouldn't love me unless I was a success.

Children like Doug, who are good students but uncertain about their identity as a good student, will show their uncertainty by trying too hard. Overcompensation always is maladaptive, and if we are to help our kids, we need to help them see what they're doing.

Children ages seven through ten have a special ability to see, acknowledge, and change unacceptable behavior when they are shown what they are doing. This ability is known as the *recognition reflex*. In facing the truth of what they are doing, they get a more realistic view about themselves—that they really are good at what they do, but they're hurting themselves by trying too hard.

Summary

Our children need an identity that they, their peers, and adults can agree on. They may be loved and welcomed into the group or hated and ostracized by them. But in either case, they achieve their identity and know where they belong.

Helping our children achieve a socially desirable identity requires tough parenting. We must use the recognition reflex to help our children see what they're doing and suggest alternative ways of achieving their identity.

But the toughest thing we are called on to do is to let our children engage in the struggle for identity *by themselves*. We should stand by to help. But only as they experience the give and take of peer relations will they find their identity in their peer group. Parents must love and accept them unconditionally as their son or daughter. But that's only part of the picture. Our kids now have to establish their place outside the home in a world that excludes us.

Socializing Forces at Work on Our Children

Psychologists use the word *socialization* to describe the process of making children well-adjusted members of the society in which they live. Three major forces influence the socialization of our children—the peer group, school, and the family. (The church can also be a force, but only to the extent that a family gets involved in a local congregation.) Let's take a look at each of these forces.

The Peer Group Because of the importance of the peer group, parents need to understand how to give their children freedom to find their place and yet not abandon their responsibility to make sure the peer group isn't a negative force. Children feel the need to conform to the group's dress code and language. They also want to impress and amaze their friends. That's what makes little boys do dangerous things. Our oldest son, Steve, now a father himself, recently told me about an incident when he and his brother David were seven and six years old. They went to after-school day care in a place that had small pebbles covering part of the yard. David would snort a pebble up his nose and spit it out his mouth. Steve was so impressed and proud of his brother that he would tell the other kids, "Come here and see what my brother can do!"

Had I known what David was doing, I would have told him how dangerous it was. Fortunately, we parents don't know a lot of the things our children do to impress their friends.

On one hand, we must recognize that impressing the peer group is a stage that our children are going through, and we need to accept it. On the other hand, we need to monitor it so they don't do it in dangerous, unacceptable ways.

If behavior is merely silly, like making faces or stretching the mouth out of shape, let it go. If it's too silly for the peer group, they'll discourage it. Even if behavior is daring, like walking along the top of a wall, don't chide your children for doing it unless they risk being badly hurt in a fall. Tough parenting permits children to run risks and learn from the bumps and bruises of life. Our job is to keep them from exceeding safe and acceptable limits.

When we do hear about the dumb or dangerous things they do, we shouldn't humiliate them ("That was a stupid thing to do") or scold them ("Never, never do that again or you'll be in big trouble"). Responses like that make our children feel we really don't understand them.

Had I known about David's stunt, I would probably have said to him and Steve, "I bet your friends really were impressed. But you need to know that's a dangerous thing to do. You could suck the pebble down your windpipe and choke to death."

We need an opportunity to evaluate the kids in our children's peer group. Having their friends come to the house to play or go out with us for pizza or to an amusement park allows us to observe the friends and see how our kids interact with them.

It's wise to know something about the parents of your children's friends. You don't have to know them personally, but you should know them over the phone. Don't be timid about calling and saying, "Ms. Jones, I'm Mary Johnson, Beth's mother. Our daughters are good friends, and I thought I would just touch base with you and let you know who I am. I'm wondering if your daughter might be able to join our family for pizza on Saturday."

This approach will give the other mother an opportunity to show an interest in getting to know a little about you, such as where you live, do you have other children, do both you and your husband work, or perhaps, are you a single-parent family like hers? Trust your intuition about this first call. What kind of feeling do you come away with? Is Ms. Jones interested in who *her* daughter's friend is, or does she sound as if she welcomes the opportunity to get rid of her daughter with no questions asked?

Sometimes children in this age group (six through ten) have a difficult time making friends because they are shy. We shouldn't push them into friendships, but we do need to let them know that other people sometimes interpret shyness as a request to be left alone.

Making friends also is difficult for children who are overweight, wear funny clothes, or have strange names. When I was in elementary school, the teacher started each day with a roll call. When she got to my name, she would hesitate, and then mispronounce it. When I would say,

"Here," I remember all the kids looking around at me quizzically, as if to say, "What is an André Bustanoby?" I was very self-conscious about my name until I was an adult.

Parents with an outgoing personality should be careful that they don't make their level of gregariousness the standard for their children. Our children may prefer to have one or two friends. It doesn't mean they're lonely, particularly when they seem to enjoy doing things by themselves or with an occasional companion. Just be sure that children who don't have the herd instinct develop adequate social skills to enable them to relate to others. Day camp, summer camp, team activities, or scouting may be ways of getting your child involved. But be careful not to push.

School School is another major socializing force. Your children's classmates and teachers create a social climate and set the tone for what is acceptable and unacceptable.

Parents should know their children's teachers. Most schools provide opportunity for parent-teacher conferences. Trust your intuition when you meet your child's teacher. How does he or she come across—high strung, tense, and irritable, or relaxed and easy to talk to? How do the teacher's perceptions of your child measure up to your own? Do you feel that he or she really knows your child and has a good grasp of child development? Does the teacher employ firm yet humane and fair means of discipline?

Some parents send their children to Christian schools, thinking that a religious education is better than a public education. It may or may not be. Several questions must be answered.

First, is this school a dumping ground for problem kids whose parents think that a good dose of Christianity will straighten them out?

Second, do the teachers have at least the same education and preparation for teaching as public school teachers?

Third, does the curriculum truly integrate the Bible with all truth? Christian teachers who don't understand that all truth is God's truth sometimes make a false distinction between the sacred and the secular, insisting that truth can be found only in the Bible. Many public school teachers, on the other hand, teach truth but cannot identify God as its ultimate source. Integrated education teaches that whatever is true (whether explicitly stated in Scripture or not) is true because God is the source. The Bible gives us *revealed* truth—any truth that we can't discover by observing nature. It comes solely by way of the Bible. But all truth is sacred and worthy of study because God is the author.

Fourth, does the school understand that children go through a human-developmental process that needs to be facilitated by parents and teachers? Or is human nature equated with the sin nature and viewed as the fleshly enemy of the spiritual life?

Unless you can have these questions answered to your satisfaction, you may not want to pay the premium for a private-school education.

Family A parent's greatest challenge as a socializing force on children of this age is being available to them without interfering. A good rule of thumb to follow is not to intervene unless there's danger of serious harm. Remember how we did it when our children were one-year-olds and they needed to develop self-confidence? Remember how we had to let them try and then stand behind them to catch them when they would fall?

The tough thing about our job now is that the bruises and bumps aren't just physical. Some are emotional. Our children feel the pain of ridicule and rejection. And yet we must let them try their hand at working through this and learning to relate to their peers.

Parenting children at this age involves not so much what we do for them as what we decide not to do. We should let them make more decisions than we ever have before.

For example, we can let them decide each day what they're going to wear. Though you may think that they should take a raincoat because it may rain or wear a jacket because it's going to be cold, let them make the decision. They probably won't take a coat, but that's okay.

Perhaps you'll say, "I don't want a sick kid on my hands." But maybe if our children get sick because of a bad decision in dressing for the day, they'll be more thoughtful the next time. The opportunity to use natural consequences to teach our children to make good decisions may be worth the inconvenience of having a sick child at home.

Tough parenting doesn't insist on having it the parents' way, particularly when permanent harm is not likely. Tough parenting sometimes means keeping our mouths shut!

Here are some pointers for giving children of this age adequate guidance:

1. *Establish boundaries.* When you put boundaries around your children, do it with a view to how much freedom you can give rather than to how tightly you can control them. Parents, afraid of losing control of their children, often don't allow enough freedom and precipitate unnecessary confrontations. Must your children make their bed and clean up their room every day before they go to school? Or

is this something you can leave up to them and just close the door if you can't stand a cluttered room?

I'm not suggesting that our children be excused from chores. But they need to be assigned and supervised in a way that minimizes confrontation (I'll have more to say about chores when I specifically discuss eight-year-olds).

Boundaries involve the kind of friends you approve of, the places they go, and what they do. The places they go and the things they do should be adjusted as they grow older.

The secret to controlling children of this age is providing consistent boundaries that give them as much space as parental prudence allows, as well as clear, firmly enforced limits to that space. This means that the boundaries aren't moved every time we get nervous about our children having too much freedom. We may need to make adjustments if we believe that we have given too much or not enough freedom, but we shouldn't get upset when our children push their limits and challenge our boundaries. Indeed, we can count on their doing it! That's the nature of children.

Some parents try to deal with pushy children by tightening the boundaries, warning their children when they have crossed them, and then resetting them at what would have been a reasonable distance to begin with. These parents feel they need to act this way in order to warn their children before things get out of hand. But this approach won't work. At some point you must stop widening the boundaries, and your children will run into an immovable wall. And they will blame you for the collision because you didn't move the wall as you usually do.

Think of the boundary of the warning track in a baseball outfield. The warning track is the wide dirt strip between the grass outfield and the outfield wall. Outfielders who are concentrating on catching a fly know they're in danger of hitting the wall when they get on the warning track. They know to stop and go no further or they'll hit the wall and get hurt.

While watching a baseball game with your kids, point out the warning track and talk with them about its function. Make the analogy between the warning track and the boundaries you set for them. Explain that you'll let them know when they're on the warning track and in danger of hitting the wall.

This approach will help us deal with children who try to get out of trouble by claiming the boundaries weren't clear. For example, you have vetoed a friendship your daughter has with another girl in the neighborhood. You have explained that you don't want her to play with the other girl anymore. You can't control their having contact at school, but when they're at home, they're not to see each other.

One day you discover that your daughter has been talking to the other girl over the phone on a regular basis. Your daughter defends herself by informing you that you said nothing about the phone. That may be true, but you can tell her that she's on the warning track. Even though you said nothing about the phone, she knows that you want her to have nothing else to do with this girl, and if she keeps going, she's going to hit the wall.

2. *Hold the line.* When you do set the boundaries, let your children know that the boundaries are not negotiable. They shouldn't be negotiable if you have set them with a view to guarding your children against serious harm.

Arguing with your children over the propriety of the boundaries only encourages them to challenge you. Our children, like the first couple in Eden, tend to focus on what they can't have rather than what they can have.

Don't be defensive or apologetic but focus on how much freedom they *do* have.

3. *Be informed.* Watch and listen. You'll find out a great deal about who your children's friends are, where they go, and what they do if you don't pry. Keeping our ears open to what the siblings are saying is a good source of information about what's going on. If you're not sure about the desirability of your kids going to a particular playground or the influence of certain kids in the neighborhood, ask the older siblings in the family what they think. They usually are very protective of little brothers and sisters and are flattered by the value you place on their opinion. Or if they're not protective, you can appeal to a baser motive. They don't want kid sister or brother to get away with things they couldn't do when they were kids, so they're happy to tell all they know.

4. *Supervise.* Be around the house, your children, and their friends as much as you can, but maintain a low profile. When your children do have friends over, you may have to insist that they not play in your child's room with the door closed if you're not sure what they're doing.

The matter of privacy is a delicate subject with children at this age. They need privacy, but they should be told that a parent's responsibility to supervise requires that we know that they're behaving themselves.

This is why children should not be permitted to have friends over to their house when no one is home or to go to a friend's house if a parent or other responsible adult isn't there. They may need to know that a teenage brother or sister isn't considered a responsible adult unless hired for the specific purpose of baby-sitting.

5. *Do fun things with your kids.* Do your kids find it fun to

be part of your family? Fun activities are a good way to get close to our children and get a sense of how they think and who their friends are.

One of the best ways to do this is to have family outings that allow the family to be together with no interference for a day or a weekend. It may be a trip to the beach, a camping trip, a day hiking, or a picnic.

Just sitting around a fire and swapping stories can give you a lot of information about your children. Often in telling about friends and activities, they reveal what they and their friends think and do. Be careful when you hear things you don't like. Don't spoil this opportunity by lecturing them. Wait for another occasion to talk about it. And don't remind them how you know about the problem. Our kids aren't aware of how much they tell about themselves when they're disarmed and chatty.

Family outings are a great time for our kids to learn about family, grandparents, and great-grandparents, where they came from, and what they did. Though our children need to fit into their peer group, understanding their roots gives them a sense of belonging to a unique, loving family that they'll always come back to even when they are adults.

Watching television together is another common family activity. Let the children select the program they want to watch. It may give you a good opportunity to talk with them about the programs they watch and help them develop thoughtful viewing habits.

Children ages six through ten enjoy fantasy themes and sitcoms involving children their own age. Talk about what goes on in the sitcoms, particularly if the behavior is rude or sarcastic. This is a good opportunity to discourage watching this kind of program and acting out the fresh behavior they see. Again, be alert to the kind of humor the show uses. Some humor is merely irreverent. For example, in the *Teenage Mutant Ninja Turtles* movie, the turtles fight for "truth, justice, and a larger slice of pizza." But most of us find the rude dialogue between Roseanne and Becky or Uncle Buck and Tia abominable. Help your kids develop discrimination by talking about the difference between acceptable humor and the sarcasm typical of so many sitcoms.

Children in this age group also enjoy watching science and nature programs. Encourage watching these programs and augment your children's viewing with video tapes of quality programs.

Individual Age Characteristics

Although the changes children make between ages six through ten are not as dramatic as those they made from birth through age five, we need to be aware of several important changes.

Age Six Age six is a transition year. Our children are getting acquainted with the world outside the home, but they haven't yet developed a sense of a peer group. Facing the world outside the home is an immense task that calls for skills the child hasn't yet developed and must develop now. This means that age six is a time of disequilibrium.

1. *School.* Our children have their first experience with the discipline of the classroom and academic expectations by teachers. Up to this point their school experience was either preschool or kindergarten, where blocks and toys were the learning tools and where the teacher read to them. Now they have to go to school a full day and begin to learn to read and write.

School pressure isn't as obvious in some children as in others. Some cry and are very verbal about their dislikes. Others say nothing but may have problems with bed-wetting, restlessness at night, or loss of appetite. Some may revert to childish behavior and begin sucking their thumb again. They may want a lot of cuddling.

Our patience with these behaviors is important. Children need to feel the security of home in order to face a world they don't understand. And sometimes they'll feign illness as an excuse to stay home. It's tough enough to deal with a child who's really sick when both parents work outside the home or when the single parent has no spouse to rely on. But we need to handle the feigned illness as carefully as the real thing.

It may be worth it to take leave time from work to nip this in the bud. The strategy is that children shouldn't be rewarded in any way when they stay home "sick." The idea we must get across to the child is this: When you say you're so sick you have to stay home, this means that you stay in bed until tomorrow morning. There will be no television, no friends over to play, no going outside, no video games. You're sick, so you stay in bed and remain quiet so you'll get over your sickness. When the rest of the family is having their regular meal, you'll have chicken soup. One or two days of this should cure feigned illness forever. If the problem becomes chronic, professional attention may be necessary.

Tough parenting of six-year-olds is parenting that expects them to tough out their introduction to the real world outside the home. But remember, it *is* a tough world, and school is no piece of cake. When they come home, don't make lots of demands of them. The pressures of school are usually all that six-year-olds can handle.

2. *Peers.* Peer relations among six-year-olds sometimes is described as a swarm. Unless it's a team game, six-year-olds don't interact with each other in the same way children do from ages seven through ten.

Just as parallel play at age three moves to play with another child at age four, play at age six moves from a swarm to a more organized group at age seven. Because of this, the influence of peers is more limited for the six-year-old than the seven-year-old. But parents will get an idea of who their children will gang up with at age seven by the kind of friends they have at age six.

3. *Fears.* It's not unusual for six-year-olds to have a problem with irrational fears. You may have thought the boogeyman was long gone. But six-year-olds are beginning to learn about the world outside of their home, and they won't always understand what they see and hear at school. Children sometimes don't ask questions because they don't want to seem dumb. Other times they don't know how to frame the question. Their questions and confusion come out in irrational fears.

We should accept these fears as a normal part of being six and listen for clues that might help us understand what's behind the fears. If children feel secure at home, particularly the security that comes from cuddling with their mom and dad, they eventually will put the fears to rest with a better understanding of their new and larger world.

Age Seven Age seven is a major step in the cognitive development of our children. By this age they have developed an ability to see the world abstractly and through the eyes of other people. The world no longer is just as they see it.

For this reason seven-year-olds tend to be more reasonable. They listen and persevere at tasks, and generally they're pleasant people.

1. *Depression.* Seven-year-olds do have down times. Un-

derstanding how other people think and having a need to fit in their peer group, seven-year-olds often feel that other kids don't like them. For example, Danny sees some kids from his class kicking around a soccer ball at the playground. He stands around, hoping they'll ask him to play too. When they don't, he comes home feeling rejected, goes to his room, and closes the door.

When you ask if everything's okay, he says "yeah," but his downcast look says otherwise. Don't pump him to find out what's wrong. Give him time to sort things out. He's probably trying to figure out what he did to deserve this rebuff, which may not have been a rebuff at all. The other kids may just have been too busy playing to pick up on Danny's desire to play too.

If Danny has developed normal social skills, he may try asking the boys if he may join them next time, braving the possibility of outright rejection. But give him time to come to this conclusion. In order for our children to master new social skills to establish themselves with their peer group, they must have time to sort things out, figure out what's wrong, and try to fix it themselves. Here we're faced with the toughest part of tough parenting—learning to let our children deal with their own hurts.

If the depression lasts for several days, we may need to intervene. The best way to intervene is not to ask the child if he's bothered about something. Let his nonverbal language speak for him. You can say, "Come here, Danny, and give me a hug." And then when Danny gives a halfhearted hug, you can say, "It looks as if you're feeling sad. I want you to know I care."

When people are hurting, the first thing they need is not advice but the assurance that someone cares. Evidence that you care can be shown in your ability to be empathic, to actually *feel* what Danny feels and voice those feelings.

Danny will probably open up to see if you really do care and may say, "The other kids don't like me."

You reply, "They don't want you hanging around with them?"

"Yeah."

"Sounds like something made you feel pushed away."

Danny would probably explain what happened, but it still would be premature to help Danny look at other reasons for their behavior or solutions to the problem. *Danny hurts and needs to feel that someone else is there with him in his hurt.*

Hug Danny and say, "It really hurts when it looks like people don't want us around. A lot of times we wonder if something's wrong with us." If you've been accurate in your assessment of Danny's feelings, Danny will feel somewhat relieved. He'll feel less lonely and isolated because you are there with him in his world of feeling. And he'll feel that he doesn't have to carry the load alone.

This doesn't mean your work is over. But it does mean that you have brought Danny back to life by empathetic human contact. After the hugs and play time, he'll feel better and be more inclined to talk.

2. *Fairness.* Seven-year-olds are very sensitive about fairness. They often feel that their friends, teachers, parents, and siblings aren't fair.

The fairness issue gives us an excellent opportunity to cultivate our children's social development. Children understand that fairness means that everyone ought to have an equal opportunity. And that's true, to a point.

For example, if all the children are sharing the same television, then each should have equal access. Older siblings have a tendency not to respect younger siblings' television time and switch channels whenever they want. This means we need rules about equal access.

But our seven-year-olds need to realize that older siblings may be permitted to watch shows that are inappropriate for the young ones, such as movies rated for thirteen-year-olds and older. Seven-year-olds need to accept your rule that they may not watch that kind of show, even if the older sibling is watching it. This introduces them to the fact that older people are permitted to do things that younger people aren't permitted to do. This is a social principle that applies not only to television but also to the places they go and the things they do.

I find that some parents, in the interest of being fair, permit their seven-year-olds to see the same television shows that their older siblings watch, even though much of the content is morally questionable. I have also seen parents in restaurants allow their young children to drink nonalcoholic "Shirley Temples" while the adults drank real cocktails. Though adults have a perfect legal and moral right to drink alcoholic beverages, including the kids in the party is inappropriate. We should be careful not to compromise our children's innocence in the name of fairness.

Age Eight In some respects eight-year-olds are like two-year-olds: They're a problem to themselves and their parents, but they don't know it. Though they're much more mature and worldly-wise, they're like two-year-olds with their speed and great energy.

1. *The age of bravado.* Eight-year-old children handle disequilibrium by pretending things don't bother them. Gone is the sensitivity of age seven. If eight-year-olds are grounded for misbehavior, they'll say, "I don't care; I didn't want to go out anyway."

Don't believe the bravado. They feel the discipline, but they're not going to give you the satisfaction of letting you know.

As I look back on the development of my own children, I realize that I made a mistake here. I had such a need to demonstrate that I was in charge, I responded badly to their indifference over my discipline. I remember telling them, "If grounding you doesn't make any difference, I bet I can find something that *will* make a difference." It usually wound up with a spanking that lasted until they let me know I won.

I really didn't win. Nobody won. I just made them angry and resentful. Because I didn't understand my insecurities as a parent, I let them hook into my need to demonstrate my power. Parents who really are in charge don't need to be angry, threatening people.

This doesn't mean that parents should permit their children to challenge their ability to discipline and make it stick. The parental mandate requires us to make our authority credible. But this isn't what we usually face with eight-year-olds. They feel the discipline but won't admit it.

2. Peer group and friends. The peer group continues to be important for the eight-year-old, but with some changes. Boys and girls begin to segregate themselves, with boys usually more verbal about not wanting to be around "stupid girls." We can't be sure why boys at this age show more aversion for girls than the other way around. Some experts suggest that boys have a more difficult time establishing their identity.

That suggestion may have some merit, and it may also help explain why boys this age tend to have such an aversion to washing themselves and wearing nice clothes. Lack of personal hygiene and clean clothes may be one of

the disgusting habits they seize on to differentiate themselves from girls.

Eight-year-olds begin to establish relationships with
good friends. The group still is important, but individual
friendships around mutual likes and interests begin to
develop.

3. *Money*. Eight-year-olds have a new fascination for
money. It may be that their cognitive development has
made them realize the place of money in getting what they
want. Until this age, their needs have been met by parents,
either in material things or in a small allowance. Suddenly
money offers them the opportunity to get what they want
without having to depend on their parents.

The problem is, their parents and other adults have the
money. How are they going to get more of it? This is a
good time to take a look at what we're teaching our
children about money. I have in mind *our attitudes*, not
just the facts of saving and being wise consumers.

Our jobs and careers don't seem like *work* to our
children. It's more like a place their parents go. My father
was a men's portrait photographer for Bachrach, the most
prestigious men's photographer in New York City. He
spent an hour or more photographing and chatting with
such luminaries as Dwight D. Eisenhower, John D.
Rockefeller, and John F. Kennedy. His work surroundings
were impressive, and I assumed that he went to lunch at
fancy restaurants like Sardis.

In short, I really didn't understand that people *work* for
their money. It wasn't until I was in high school and heard
my dad arguing with my mom over how she spent money
that I realized how much pressure he felt.

I then began to notice that from Thanksgiving to
Christmas, the busiest season at work, he came home
looking like death warmed over. I think it was then that I

developed my work ethic and realized that money meant sacrifice and pressure. I felt sad that I hadn't understood sooner what it cost my dad to provide for us.

I'm not suggesting that we burden our children with our work pressures and create in them feelings of insecurity. But I do think that we must be careful not to act as if the work world is glamorous and not to suggest by our spending habits that money comes easily.

Establishing an allowance policy may help eight-year-olds develop a more realistic view of money. Give them a modest allowance of a couple of dollars a week to spend as they wish, but if they want more, they need to work for it. Doing jobs for us, over and above their usual chores, such as yard work or washing the car, can go a long way to help them understand that they don't get more money unless they produce. And if they don't have the money to satisfy their wants, they have a choice: do without or work for it. That's tough parenting.

Allowance shouldn't be payment for chores. We create unnecessary difficulty for ourselves when we do this. Suppose the rule is they get no allowance if they don't do their chores. They may opt not to do their chores and do without.

An allowance is a modest grant for discretionary purchases. We should make it clear to them what we expect their allowance to be spent for. For example, when the family goes to the movies, do we expect them to buy their own snacks or is this part of the family outing? If it's the rule that they buy their own, we should be ready to say no to a request for soda or popcorn.

The purpose of the allowance is to let our children know that their wants are infinite but the money to satisfy them is not. They learn this only by experience, and tough parenting means that there are no "freebees" when the allowance is gone.

Chores are expected of children because they're members of the family. Membership in a family has both its costs and benefits, an important social lesson that prepares them for adulthood and the establishment of their own families.

Age Nine We have seen how our children's development goes in cycles of equilibrium and disequilibrium. Though they may handle it differently, eight- and nine-year-olds both are in disequilibrium. Eight-year-olds are very outward; nine-year-olds are more inward. Eight-year-olds will rebel by being indifferent to discipline; nine-year-olds will rebel by complaining.

1. *The complainer.* Because nine-year-olds complain so much, age nine is sometimes called a neurotic age. Nine-year-olds feel "sick" a great deal, but usually it's when they're asked to do something they don't want to do. One way to deal with their excuses is to let them know that if they're so sick they can't do their chores, then they're too sick to go out and play with their friends.

One complaint that we should pay attention to is difficulty with reading. When reading disability surfaces, it often happens at age nine. It may appear in connection with a great deal of worry over failing in school. Special tutoring and perhaps some special testing for reading problems should be done.

2. *The worrier.* Not only are nine-year-olds complainers, they're also worriers. Some of their worries may be legitimate, particularly if those worries are connected with reading problems. But many of nine-year-olds' worries are the result of their stage of development. As their cognitive skills and social awareness develop, nine-year-olds become aware of many things that they feel powerless to do

anything about or they don't yet have the social skill to handle.

For example, the peer group is an important part of our children's lives at this age. But other kids can be mean in the way they form cliques and exclude our children or in the way they taunt them and hurt their feelings. We must be careful not to rush in when our children are hurt or fret about the way they're being treated by their friends.

3. *Talking to nine-year-olds.* Being available to talk when our children worry is important. But we must not *insist* that they talk to us about it; if we do, they'll shut us out all the more. They need to know that we are receptive and nonjudgmental when they do talk. Rather than rush in with solutions, it's wiser to tune in to their complaints and their worry. Only when they feel us with them emotionally will they open up to our guidance.

4. *Personality and temperament.* Our children's personality and temperament may be part of their problem with their peers. By age nine, our children begin to emerge as unique people. Do they have particularly offensive traits that we see when they're with their friends? Do they alienate their friends with bossy or hostile behavior? Or do they set themselves up to be picked on by being too docile or ingratiating?

Don't try to orchestrate your children's social responses by telling them exactly what to do, because the solution may not fit every situation. Try not to put personality or temperament labels on them as if they're indelibly stamped with traits that can't change.

Address the behavior. You may say, for example, "Michelle, I notice when you're with your girlfriends that you sometimes sound nasty when you talk to them. I wonder if this has anything to do with how they treat you?"

Michelle may deny that she's nasty to her friends or to anyone else. But at least you'll have sown a seed idea.

5. *Fairness.* Nine-year-olds continue their concern for fairness. Parents will become irritated with their complaints because they don't see how unfair *they* can be, particularly in the way they treat us. We should be careful not to lash out, however. We can let them know that we feel treated unfairly when they won't do their chores but still expect us to do things for them.

Pam's mother feels this way and says to her daughter, "Pam, I hear a lot of talk about how unfairly I treat you. You're mad because I won't drop everything and take you to the store to buy a new pair of shoes. I need you to know that I really feel taken for granted and used. I asked you fifteen minutes ago to empty the wastebaskets, and you didn't do it. Now you want me to stop what I'm doing and take you to the store. Do you understand the problem I have with that?"

Pam most likely will be angry and defensive. She'll probably go to her bedroom and pout. But don't worry; her mother probably got through at some level.

6. *Hobbies and lessons.* Eight- and nine-year-olds are very similar in their interest in hobbies and lessons, especially music lessons. Be patient with them about both interests. Though nine-year-olds have an ability to persevere, they do have their limits. They haven't yet developed the ability to pace themselves, and when they're done, they just drop what they're doing.

With hobbies, this can mean a constantly messy house. For example, model builders will leave parts, tools, and debris scattered all around. If we expect our children to clean up and put things away every time they're done, we'll discourage the interest. Give them a space of their own where they can leave the mess. If your house is small and you don't like to see the mess, just keep the door closed.

Nine-year-olds often approach music lessons the same way they approach hobbies. They can persevere, but when they're done, they're done. Let them establish their own time and length of practice, though you might want to have them agree to a bare minimum. Don't kill the interest by pushing them beyond their endurance. Most instruments can be rented, even pianos. It might be wise to rent rather than buy until the child shows serious dedication. Or else purchase an inexpensive, used instrument or a simple electronic keyboard.

Also, keep alert to reasons why the child may be losing interest. Make sure you have selected the child's teacher carefully and that you approve of the music training theory. Take time to understand the variety of teaching approaches available, and choose the one you think best fits your child's temperament.

7. *Pets.* Nine-year-olds love pets. But pets are treated like hobbies and musical instruments—lots of intense interest, from time to time. But pets need more consistent, regular treatment than hobbies and instruments.

Don't get a pet for the child to own and care for. You'll wind up with the majority of care. Let it be a family pet with shared responsibility. Pets shouldn't suffer from a child's irresponsibility, and children shouldn't suffer from unnecessary parental hassles.

Summary

Age nine is still friends oriented, though nine-year-olds also enjoy going on outings with their parents. Don't let their ambivalence about a family outing discourage you from encouraging and planning it. Outings with nine-year-

olds still offer us opportunities to cultivate our relationship.

Tough parenting is a discipline for parents as well as
children. We aren't always appreciated for what we do, and
at this age, we may begin to feel our children growing away
from us. The people and the world away from home are
gaining more and more attraction for them. But that's the
way it should be.

Age Ten

Most parents report that ten-year-olds are enjoyable
people to be around. It's true that they tend to be tolerant
and easygoing, except toward younger siblings who pester
them and get into their room. But the main reason why
parents like ten-year-olds is that *ten-year-olds actually
believe our word is law!*

Ten-year-olds have developed enough cognitively and
socially to realize that their parents really do know a great
deal about a lot of things. As a result, ten-year-olds are
willing to listen and learn from parents and teachers as
never before.

This is a time of equilibrium, which is another reason
for the child to be more relaxed. It's also a milestone.
Children at this age have achieved what they began at age
six—finding out how they fit into the world outside the
family. By now they have achieved some sense of who they
are and how other people see them.

Because of their age and agreeability, this is a good time
to deal with the important subjects of sex and drugs. It's
not that these subjects shouldn't be discussed before this
time, but we are able to be more direct with the receptive
ten-year-old.

1. *Talking about sex.* If you are a parent who has neglected

talking to your children about sex for whatever reason, here are a couple of things you can do.

First, don't feel rushed to give them a crash course on the subject. You still have a little time, like when they're eleven or twelve years old.

Second, if anything in your past hinders you from talking to your children about sex, come to terms with it. It may be that growing up in a sexually repressed (or sexually loose) atmosphere has influenced your attitudes about sex far more than you realize. You may even have avoided answering simple questions your children have asked over the years or have answered them in ways that left your children feeling as if they shouldn't have asked the question.

Third, browse through your local bookstore and find books about sexual development, books both for your children to read for themselves and for you to read and share with them.

Fourth, if you feel that you've been silent on the subject over the years, don't be afraid to let your child know that you've neglected something in their education and that you feel it's important to talk together about sexual matters.

You can open the subject by giving the child something to read and saying, "I'd like you to read this, and when you're done, I'd like to talk about it." Don't leave it up to your child to open the subject again. You'll have to do it.

When you do talk, you'll find that the facts are easy enough to talk about. Go over them and make sure that your child has accurate information. Because they're approaching puberty, it's important that boys know about wet dreams and girls know about menstruation. Your daughter should know that you'll soon provide the necessary sanitary aids. If you're a single parent and your child is of the opposite sex, you may want a close friend or relative of the opposite sex to help you.

Our children should know more than just the mechanics of sexual intercourse. They need to know that it's a wonderful thing that happens between a husband and a wife who love each other very much.

You'll want to say something about masturbation to both your son and daughter. Whatever your view about the morality of masturbation, don't make your child fearful of medical or emotional consequences. There is no scientific evidence to support the raising of such fears. Though people with physical or emotional sexual problems may masturbate, it wasn't masturbating that created the problem. However, if you have reason to believe your child is masturbating frequently, it could be a sign of deeper emotional distress. Talking with a psychologist may be in order.

The most difficult thing will be to get a sense of your children's attitudes toward sex. Not long ago kids this age didn't talk much about *who* to have sex with but rather they would sneak dirty magazines or movies and giggle at body parts. But with the loss of innocence, sexual behavior has changed to the point that even ten-year-olds are starting to talk about who they want to have sex with.

If you aren't sure how advanced your children are on the subject, rather than ask them what *their* attitudes are, ask what the kids their age are talking about. For example you can ask, "When other kids talk about sex, do they think it's okay to have sex with someone you're not married to?" As long as you're asking what the *other* kids think, you're safe. And you're probably safe in believing your children feel that way too, unless they say otherwise.

If you pick up sexual attitudes that trouble you, don't start lecturing. If you do, your child will never talk about sex again. Look for opportunities on other occasions to address the subject and advance your ideas. You may have an opportunity as you watch a television program together. When the program is over, talk about it. But again, don't lecture or preach. You can say, "I feel troubled when I see people have sex and they're not married. If I'd done that, I'd really feel crummy."

This would also be a good time to talk about AIDS. Most sex as portrayed on television doesn't handle the subject of safe sex. It's usually portrayed as a very spontaneous, romantic episode. A simple observation that they didn't deal with the problem of safe sex would be in order. Or you may raise the question, "How did they know they weren't running the risk of getting AIDS?"

2. *Talking about drugs.* We should create a home atmosphere that doesn't send a double message about the use of drugs.

First, what's your attitude about prescription drugs? Tranquilizers may sometimes be used temporarily until we can muster our coping skills, and though antidepressants such as Prozac need to be taken on a longer term by some people, we must all be careful not to talk as if we couldn't make it through life without our pills.

Second, if you drink alcoholic beverages, what kind of attitude do your children pick up? Whether you say it or not, they may get the message that you can't wait to have a drink. If your children see you frequently resort to alcohol to solve pressure problems, they may think that's how life is supposed to be. The drug of choice today is alcohol. If you use it and have it at home, you may want to be sure that it's out of your children's reach.

Kids also need to know that all drugs (including alcohol) that are regulated by law stipulate that minors are forbidden to use them.

Browse through your bookstore and find drug-related books appropriate for your children. After reading them and having your child read them, discuss the issues together. Don't deny that drugs may feel good temporarily, but talk with your kids about the price a person pays for that good feeling.

Summary

If you are listening to your kids, monitoring their friendships and the places they go, you'll develop a sense of what's going on. It's too much to expect our kids to come to us and tell us that they're experimenting with drugs or alcohol. But if they know that we listen to concerns and handle their mistakes without lecturing or overreacting, they'll be less secretive and problem behavior will be more visible.

The "mystery years" need not be a mystery if we're keeping our eyes and ears open. Don't pry, but be available to talk and spend time with your kids. When they feel that we're not preoccupied with more important things and we regard our relationship with them as important, we'll even surprise ourselves by how much we really can know about them and influence them.

The toughest thing about tough parenting in the mystery years is resisting the impulse to fix things. Much parenting that goes on in these years allows our children to work through the tough job of finding their place in the world without our interference.

8

Good-bye Childhood:
Ages Eleven and Twelve

Preadolescence is to childhood what childhood is to infancy: a time of detachment from parents. Disequilibrium and disharmony are the norm. Though we enjoyed our ten-year-olds, they have to get on with growing up.

Understanding the Changes in Preadolescents

Preadolescence is the breaking up of childhood, and especially of the feeling that adults are allies and that adults know what they're talking about. Eleven- and twelve-year-olds go through a great deal of psychological, physical, and academic change.

Preadolescence is a good name for this stage because children are not yet adolescents; but they also are no longer children. This in-betweenness makes preadolescence especially difficult for both children and parents. The old behaviors of childhood no longer fit, and the new behaviors of adolescence haven't yet been mastered.

Psychological Changes The two most radical psychological changes parents notice in preadolescents are *rebellion* and *depression*.

1. Rebellion. Remember the terrible twos—when you said yes, your child said no—or vice versa? The conflict at that time came from our children's awareness that they were not an extension of their mother. They realized they were individuals, and they went through a process of separation and individuation.

Preadolescents go through a similar process. They're leaving childhood to become more mature persons. They like to think that the new identity is adulthood. But if we think of it as non-childhood, we may find this new stage easier to handle.

Preadolescents develop a *negative* identity before they achieve a *positive* identity. They're not sure of what they want, but they know they must break from the past. And they feel a need to reject whatever ties them to it. Most often this break with the past is expressed in conflict with their parents.

When preadolescents tell us they're not children any-more, we parents sometimes respond sarcastically, "Sure, sure. Eleven going on twenty-two!"

Then we begin a fruitless argument with, "Well, if you're so grown up, then tell me this . . ." If pressed, they'll come up with all sorts of responses and defend their ideas vigorously. Everyone loses in a confrontation like this. The issue isn't who knows more about adulthood. The issue is preadolescents' *emotional* distancing from their childhood and the people who represent it—their parents. Our kids aren't adults; but they're also not children.

Sometimes our kids will bait us to create more distance. Bruce's parents are sending him to Christian Academy so he will not be influenced by the humanism and secularism of public school. One evening at supper Bruce announced that he was going to write a paper about evolution because his science teacher at school was putting it down.

His parents could have saved themselves unnecessary worry if they recognized that Bruce was trying to find his own way to adulthood by sorting out important issues for himself. Instead of arguing about creationism and evolution, Bruce's parents could have stimulated the educational process by studying the issues and listening to Bruce talk about his findings in a non-attacking, nondefensive way.

2. *Depression*. Preadolescents aren't aware of it, but they are in a period of mourning. Though they have a strong need to break with the past, they experience an important loss. Their relationship with their parents is different. Though parents are still happy to have their eleven-year-olds cuddle, preadolescents have ambivalent feelings about childlike needs and don't understand them. Their moods often swing between dependence and independence.

These feelings are depressing, and it's not unusual for preadolescents to be belligerent. When we ask, "Is anything wrong?" they'll retort, "Nothing's wrong!"

Tough parenting avoids becoming overly alarmed at this behavior and avoids the urge to fix whatever's wrong. A parent can't fix this emotional molting any more than the mother crab can fix the loss of her offspring's shell.

Our task is to stand by and provide a secure, consistent atmosphere for the child and not take personally the belligerence we sometimes get from our children. They're going through a struggle to give up their childhood.

We can be on the lookout for signs that they aren't coping well. Do they have more bad days than good ones? How quickly do they bounce back from disappointment?

Remember that this was one of the ways you could tell how distressed your baby was. When comforted, did your baby's tears dry up quickly? Or did they continue to flow? We can't comfort preadolescents as we do babies. But do they respond reasonably quickly to loving support?

Raising preadolescents is much like teaching children to swim. The easiest way to teach children to swim is to let them spend a great deal of time playing in a lake or bay where the water is calm and the slope of the shore is gradual. Let them play in the shallows where they can fall in, get their faces wet, and even go underwater unexpectedly. They'll gain experience in putting their faces underwater this way. Let them go as deep as they want, as long as you're standing by to help if necessary.

We really don't teach our children to swim. They teach themselves to swim while they explore this exciting new freedom of being in the water. We stand by to keep them from serious trouble. They need the security of our presence, but they need to prove to themselves, and us, that they can take care of themselves. Wise parents don't point out how important their protection is. Instead, they maintain an unobtrusive presence and exude a confidence that says, "You can do it."

Physical Changes In addition to the many emotional changes a preadolescent feels are the many physical changes that accompany this stage. Child-development specialists are unsure how directly hormonal changes influence the mood swings of preadolescents, but they do know that the development of distinctly male and female characteristics affects the way preadolescents feel about themselves.

Early maturation is an advantage for boys. They appear more masculine than late-developing boys. The opposite is the case for girls. Early-developing girls appear self-conscious about their bodies while late-maturing girls are more confident and poised.

In girls, the uterus and ovaries begin to develop at about age nine or ten. Well-developed pubic hair signals the start of vaginal secretion and pelvic growth. Breast development begins to show by age ten or eleven. Menarche (first menstruation) occurs at about age twelve-and-a-half. At age thirteen, nipples show pigmentation, and breasts show further growth.

Girls are about two years ahead of boys in their development. A late-maturing boy and an early-maturing girl of the same age can be as much as *four years* apart in their development. This can produce tremendous conflict in both the girl and the boy. The girl may be embarrassed because she doesn't look like her peers. The boy feels embarrassed for the same reason. And he looks even more immature when compared with the girl.

The secretion of male hormones usually begins in boys at age eleven-and-a-half with the onset of growth spurts at ages twelve, thirteen, and fourteen. Noticeable growth in the penis occurs during this period. Their first wet dream happens at about age twelve. Voice change comes at about age fourteen-and-a-half or fifteen, when the larynx enlarges and the vocal cords lengthen. Full height is achieved at about age eighteen.[1]

Late-developing boys sometimes compensate for their slower physical development by becoming overly compliant with their peers or by engaging in bravado or aggressive and risk-taking behavior. We may attempt to assure them they'll catch up with the other kids, but it probably won't help.

The boy who overcompensates with aggression gets little sympathy. But he does need our patience. He often does well in sports because he has the drive necessary to perform physically. Encourage him in the direction of sports that suit his physique. For example, if he's long and gangly for his age, he might make a good swimmer. Short, well-proportioned boys may do well in gymnastics. The small, light boy may do well in weight-classed wrestling. If your son's school doesn't offer these opportunities, look for boys' clubs that do. An investment of time and money may help your son through a difficult period.

Sports also help girls compensate for their physical size. Well-developed girls may use their size to advantage in basketball or softball. Smaller girls may find gymnastics or figure skating suitable.

Sometimes late-developing children have interests and skills that other kids don't have, which makes them a "cut above" in their own way. For example, do they show musical, artistic, or computer skills that can be cultivated? Compensation is a primary method children use to make up for real or imagined differences. They learn that they don't have to be just like everyone else to gain respect.

When we encourage our children, we must be careful not to give them the idea that their personal worth or value is based on their performance. We need to convey the message that they are okay even if they don't play sports or don't prove to be the best of anything. We can communicate our unconditional feeling of worth by spontaneously hugging them and saying, "I'm glad you're my kid!" Our children don't have to do anything but just be themselves to deserve our attention and affection.

Another physical change—acne—affects how preadolescents see themselves. Because children's body-image is so important at this age, we should look for early signs of acne (more common in boys than girls), especially if it's known to run in the family. Acne occurs when hair follicles, plugged with oily secretions, breed bacteria.[2] If your children encounter much more than a few pimples and blackheads, take them to a doctor for professional treatment. Picking and squeezing the infection may result in spreading and scarring.

Academic Changes As if psychological and physical changes were not enough, our children also face an important academic change. Eleven- and twelve-year-olds leave the security of elementary school and enter middle school (grades six through eight in many areas) or junior high school (grades seven through eight or nine in many areas). In this new academic setting, they're expected to be more independent, to motivate themselves to study. If they don't do the work, school goes on without them.

A large part of the problem preadolescents have with school is a lack of connection between the subject matter and life as they experience it. What is needed are teachers who can establish rapport and encourage the aptitude of the child.

This connectedness was beautifully portrayed by Robin Williams in the movie *Dead Poets' Society.* One would think that nothing would be more boring to boys than poetry. Yet, the teacher Williams portrayed brought poetry to life for his students. He was excited about the subject, and his rapport with the students made poetry a living thing they could all share.

Teachers may find it difficult to establish rapport with sixth and seventh graders, but they must try if they are to educate preadolescents. Students sense when a teacher knows where they are individually and collectively, is vitally interested in them, and wants to share the excitement of the subject with them.

Interest or aptitude testing may help you and your school give your child direction and encouragement. And parent-child-teacher conferences may give you a sense of the rapport the teacher has with your child.

If your child can't make connections with the teacher in school, you might consider getting a tutor—perhaps a university student whose age may be a special asset. If the first tutor doesn't connect with your child, try another one.

Youth pastors often have a good rapport with kids, usually because they like kids and they like their work. If your church has a youth pastor, you may want to get his or her view of your child. Other people often can see things that we are too close to see. The youth pastor's insight may give us some clues about what's going on and how the child might be reached in school.

Television Viewing Kids like to see stories about people their own age. The Disney Channel and the Discovery Channel offer some good family programming.

As we discussed before with younger children, we must decide, especially with sitcoms, where irreverent humor ends and rudeness begins. If your kids insist on watching programs that you feel are marginal, watch with them and talk about what you like and don't like about the programs, especially the behavior and language of the parents and kids. And don't be afraid to veto programs you find inappropriate.

Age Characteristics

An important difference between ages eleven and twelve is that age twelve is a more mellow, less abrasive time than age eleven. This difference translates into everything eleven- and twelve-year-olds do.

Attitudes

Eleven-year-olds Eleven-year-olds act as if they don't have a problem. And, indeed, they believe that if parents and siblings weren't so difficult to get along with, life at home would be much easier.

Parents who have been just barely managing to keep control up to this point are in danger of losing it by caving in to the intimidation eleven-year-olds can dish out. Some parents lose it by giving up whenever their child gets ugly. This encourages eleven-year-olds to test further to see if they really have gained the upper hand.

Single, overburdened mothers with eleven-year-old boys are in special danger. Tired of trying to hold the line by themselves, they often give up. Mothers with physically or emotionally absent husbands are in the same danger. They have no one to strengthen their resolve.

Another way parents lose the battle of control is by developing a bad attitude toward their eleven-year-olds. They become just as obnoxious as their children and prove it by out-screaming their kids.

It's at this point that kids learn to play Uproar, a game played by a child and one or more parents. The object is to distract the parent from the real issue, such as fighting with a sibling, lying, stealing, or backtalk. Children achieve the goal by escalating obnoxious behavior beyond their parents' endurance. They'll know that they have achieved their goal when their parents explode. The child's strategy at this point is to retreat into shocked indignation, possibly even with tears, and to say something like, "I can't believe you said those terrible things to me!" The goal is to make parents forget what the fracas was all about by getting them to wallow in the guilt of having said all those awful things.

Uproar game can be refined endlessly until the child is old enough to leave home and the parents are thoroughly dispirited and cowed. Unless, of course, they are tough parents.

Tough parents aren't screamers. They are in control of their emotions.

By the time children are preadolescents, their parents find that spanking is unnecessary because they're able to control their children with things like grounding or restricting the use of television and the telephone. But what about children who ignore the restrictions and continue to do as they please. What then? Kids like this are starting to get out of hand. Handling these kinds of situations is discussed more fully in chapter 12.

If you do spank, do so only as a last resort. And when you're done, send them the message, verbally and nonverbally, that you're ready for reconciliation when they are. Reinforce the reconciliation with a hug. Above all, don't lecture.

Twelve-year-olds Twelve-year-olds are disarming, given the experience we had with them when they were eleven-year-olds. Comparatively, they can be charmers. Your daughter may say, "Would I ever disobey a wonderful mother like you?" She'll say it with a smile and a teasing tone of voice, but you'll find it hard not to be disarmed. Let her know that you're willing to play the game, but you do know what she's doing. Smile and say, "Yeah, yeah; your charm will get you everywhere."

There's a subtle message in that reply. On one hand, you reinforce her socially acceptable response. Yet on the other hand, you're warning her not to push it.

Lies

Lies are another behavior that eleven- and twelve-year-olds handle differently.

Eleven-year-olds Eleven-year-olds often find that trustworthiness, a dimly understood abstraction, gets in the way of saving their skin. The practical consequences of not being trustworthy really haven't sunk in.

When their honesty is questioned, eleven-year-olds vehemently defend it, whether or not they really have lied. This, of course, presents a problem to parents. Is this child trustworthy? If the child has a history of untrustworthiness, a pall will hang over the incident until the truth is known or forgotten.

A child's untrustworthiness erodes the parent-child relationship. And though the child may not understand the estrangement created by a lie, dealing with a lie is a good opportunity to explain what's happening without accusing. We can say something like, "Karen, I know that you want me to believe your story. But I'm having a hard time. And the reason I can't believe it is that you've lied about this before. So even if you're telling me the truth now, I really can't be sure." An important lesson is taught by this response. If Karen *is* telling the truth, she has only herself to blame for her parents not believing her.

Trustworthiness creates trust. What's more, lies usually create a problem bigger than the one the child is trying to avoid. It is a breach in the relationship of people who live with and love each other. People who live in close proximity to each other must feel they can trust each other. Explaining this to your eleven-year-old may not yield a confession of truth. But it will help your child understand the *real* consequences of lying.

One parent asked me, "So what do you do when you catch a child in a lie? Ignore it?"

No, parents shouldn't ignore the lie. Instead, they should explain to the child that lying damages trust, and puts emotional distance between child and parent. Parents are then less likely to believe them and more ready to check up on them. An atmosphere of suspicion poisons the relationship. Because children want to be trusted, they find this a very uncomfortable position to be in, and often that is enough to deter further lying.

However, if your child continues to lie, parents may need to set new rules in those areas where the child tends to lie. For example, if your daughter lies about the places she goes with her friends, you may need to forbid her from seeing those friends.

Twelve-year-olds Twelve-year-olds, on the other hand, may not be more trustworthy than eleven-year-olds, but if they value their relationship to you, they won't want to disrupt it by lying.

Notice the caveat: *If they value their relationship to you.* Does your consistent, thoughtful, loving behavior help your child value his or her relationship to you?

I question the effectiveness of punishing children for lying. If a breach in their relationship to their parents isn't enough to correct the problem, we have a problem that goes beyond lying, a problem that may need professional help. Perhaps the problem is a dysfunctional family or lack of impulse control in the child. Children who show lack of impulse control not only seem unable to control their impulses such as lying but also seek gratification by indulging the impulse.

Tough parenting is firm but not harsh with the lying child. Control of our own anger or our disappointment in the child is important. We must send our children the message that our concern is for *them*. Parents with high moral values run the risk of leaving the impression that the moral code is more important than the child who has violated it.

Chores

If you haven't already had conflicts with your children over chores, you will. Preadolescents are big enough to carry some of their own weight, and this is the time to develop their responsibility for certain tasks, if you haven't done so already.

Eleven-year-olds Eleven-year-olds can make parents feel taken for granted. On one hand, they expect all the amenities of family life, but on the other, they can be indifferent to contributing anything in return.

We may be able to keep our composure by remembering that the task of the preadolescent is to make a break from childhood and everything that represents it. Our children's dependence on us to feed, clothe, and house them is a constant reminder that they're stuck with us for a while. To one degree or another, this tension between needing us and not wanting to need us will continue until they leave home.

We would think that children who are asked to do chores would do them gladly as evidence that they're carrying some of their own weight and aren't totally dependent on us. But the logic doesn't work that way. Prisoners of war don't gladly contribute to the efficiency of the POW camp. They have only one thing on their mind: escape.

Perhaps you'll say, "Come on, now. Home life isn't that bad for my kids. In fact, they have it pretty good." I believe you. But remember, our children's task is to grow away from us. Chores are a reminder that they still are bound to home and family. And when we try to motivate them by saying, "You're part of this family too," we only make matters worse.

When it comes to getting your children to do chores, first try the direct approach and give them jobs such as taking out the trash, cutting the grass, or shoveling snow. If you get resistance, you can try a second approach.

Passive resistance on the part of the child, such as, "I forgot," can be met with passive resistance on the part of the parent. You can "forget" too. You can forget to iron the blouse your daughter wanted to wear to school the next day. You can forget to take your son to soccer practice or just not be around when he needs transportation. I've had parents say they can't do such a thing, but they'll continue to fume and fuss when their children evade their chores. Tough parenting means keeping your cool and being imaginative in the battle of wits with your children.

Your eleven-year-old will catch on quickly, and in accusatory tones say, "You didn't forget—you did that deliberately!" Keep your sense of humor, and play it to the hilt: "I'm hurt and offended by such a suggestion. Why should I forget to do something you wanted me to do?" Let the child think about the full implications of your stunt before you make your point. Perhaps he or she won't even need further explanation.

Our children need to learn that life is full of trade-offs. They may not be willing to do chores because they're part of the family, but they may be willing to do them if they want something from their parents.

Twelve-year-olds Twelve-year-olds are quite responsive to the parental-irresponsibility gambit because they have a sense of humor. Eleven-year-olds are infuriated when we beat them at their own game; twelve-year-olds might even laugh about it.

Though twelve-year-olds won't volunteer to do anything, they're a little more agreeable when asked. It may help to have a specific day and time for their chores. Write them down and post them in a conspicuous place. Make it clear that the chores are to be done before the children are allowed to play outside or go anywhere.

When my children were preadolescents and teenagers, we had a rule that their rooms had to be cleaned up every

Saturday before they did anything else. We were specific about what clean meant, and the room had to pass inspection before they could go out. If they planned to go anywhere on Saturday, we reminded them that they better get up early enough to do it and not sleep till the last minute before they had to go. If they had nowhere to go, sometimes the job would drag on for hours, with several failed inspections.

The two older boys shared a room and would argue over who was to pick up what. We would hear arguments like, "That's not my chewing-gum wrapper on the floor!" When they would complain about lack of cooperation from the other one, we would tell them they would have to work it out.

It was amazing how quickly and thoroughly they could do the job when they realized that half the day was gone and they still weren't able to go outside or that their friends were waiting for them to get done. Tough parenting under these circumstances must be persistent, consistent, and calm.

Relating to the Opposite Sex

Relating to the opposite sex is different not only between eleven- and twelve-year-olds but also between boys and girls. Girls tend to be more advanced than boys in their opposite-sex interest. Eleven-year-old boys are just beginning to come into puberty, while the twelve-year-old boy usually has his first experience with masturbation or wet dreams.

Girls are more interested in tender feelings and romance, while boys are more interested in the female body and the sex organs. This is why boys are far more interested in pornography. This isn't unusual. And though I believe in forbidding pornography, I also know that boys *will* find some way to gratify their interest in the female body.

Before pornographic magazines existed, boys perused art books, the lingerie sections of the Sears catalog, and pictures of unclad natives in *National Geographic*. Though this behavior may be reprehensible to mothers, it may be helpful if you look at it as doing their job as boys— developing interest in the female body. You certainly wouldn't want them *not* to be interested!

Twelve-year-old boys show more overt interest in girls than eleven-year-old boys, though eleven-year-old boys do fantasize about girls. They show their interest by teasing, and they experience their first physical contact by pushing and pulling, and the girls respond by hitting them—all in fun.

Girls show their interest in boys by responding good-naturedly to the torment by boys and by sending messages through friends that they like a certain boy.

Interest in the opposite sex is normal in preadolescence, and parents ought to handle it in a matter-of-fact manner and neither encourage nor discourage it. Though a boy or girl may think of someone as a girlfriend or boyfriend, pairing off at this age shouldn't be encouraged. At this age, it's enough for boys and girls to get acquainted with their interest in the opposite sex without pursuing it further. They aren't yet emotionally ready for the deep feelings that develop from a dating and love relationship and the romantic and sexual urges that pairing off encourages.

Preadolescents are just making their break from childhood. If we can successfully navigate that hazard, we'll have helped our kids take a major step toward maturity. We must not rush the rest of their adolescence. Remember, for everything there's a season.

Tough parenting during these years actually can be fun. Our children are beginning to think more like adults, and we are more able to deal with them on that level. Rather than see your preadolescents as children who are getting too big to control physically, look at it as a challenge—an opportunity to show adult wit that they are no match for. Not only will it win the day for you, it will give your kids a new respect for you.

9

Helping Them Become Adolescents: Age Thirteen

The teenage years can be the most enjoyable phase for both parents and their kids. By now our children have become unique people with their own personalities, and they're beginning to relate to us on an adult level. They quickly sense unconditional parental love that says in both word and deed, "I'm glad you're my kid, not for anything you do, but just because you are you." We'll have our times of disagreement, and we may have to exercise the parental mandate. But most teenagers respond agreeably to people who make them feel accepted.

If we look at age thirteen as an opportunity for a great adventure with our kids, we'll find that we can be very positive in our guidance. Age thirteen is a transition between preadolescence (ages eleven and twelve) and adolescence (ages fourteen through seventeen). Our task as parents of thirteen-year-olds is to prepare them for independence and the emotional sorrow and joy that goes with it—the loss of home and family and the establishment of their own life and relationships.

The idea of coming and going at will and pursuing their interests with a minimum of parental interference sounds good to them, and most thirteen-year-olds feel they're ready for it. It takes a great deal of patience to help them understand that with independence comes the responsibility to provide for their own financial and emotional support. And that's difficult to do when they've always depended on their parents to satisfy these needs.

Take for example the benefits of living at home: shelter that's warm in the winter and cool in the summer, electricity to play the television and stereo, clothes to wear, a bed to sleep in, access to the rest of the house when needed, food on the table and an endless supply in the refrigerator and cupboards to share with their friends, education, allowance, transportation, dues and fees for clubs and sports teams, medical and dental care, protection from harm and unreasonable demands from outside the family, the status of a minor before the law, protection from poor decisions, and emotional support.

Telling our kids that they can't have the best of two lives—the life of dependence on parents and a life of independence—doesn't help them understand the task ahead. Never having had to provide all these things for themselves and seldom having had to do without, thirteen-year-olds are unable to set a value on them or imagine what it would be like to do without or provide for themselves.

Our task with thirteen-year-olds is to help them understand what independence means and what they'll be expected to cope with from age fourteen on. Age thirteen is a time when we say to our kids, "On your mark, get set . . ."

Making Our Expectations Clear

Thirteen-year-olds need to know what we'll be expecting of them over the next four years. But making our expectations clear doesn't happen simply by sitting down with them and having a talk, although a talk is certainly appropriate, particularly when our children voice concerns about the future.

As with most education at home, talking about our expectations will need to occur as the conversation naturally lends itself to the subject. For example, if your child talks about dating, that is a good time to explain your expectations about dating and activities with peers.

Making your expectations clear also means that you have thought through how you intend to facilitate your adolescent's becoming physically and emotionally independent and able to establish stable relationships. You will need to discuss some of the following subjects with your adolescent.

Leaving Home Though we don't expect kids at this tender age to be ready to leave home, we need to get them used to the idea that they soon will be facing this prospect, possibly within their next four or five years.

Parents and mental-health professionals lament the fact that today's young people have a protracted adolescence. Their adult independence is delayed by economic conditions that make it unaffordable or a technical society that requires a high degree of education—something that takes time and money.

Economics and education are indeed factors that make growing up nowadays difficult, but they are by no means the fundamental cause of the problem. I believe the root cause is *a lack of tough parenting.*

Tough parents of thirteen-year-olds should tell them, "You want to grow up and be independent; we want you to grow up and be independent. These are some things that we'll be expecting of you in order to accomplish that goal. The first is that you understand our rule about leaving home. We expect you to graduate from high school, and then we'll give you four more years at home to get either a college or vocational education so you can earn a decent living. If you choose not to go on for further education, we expect you to move out, get a job, and support yourself."

When parents hear this, they may reply, "That's absolutely unrealistic. Seventeen- or eighteen-year-old high-school graduates can't support themselves in these times."

Try putting it this way: "Seventeen- or eighteen-year-old high-school graduates can't support themselves in the manner to which they have become accustomed."

Thirteen-year-olds don't think about the cost of living and the kind of money they'll have to earn to continue their comfortable lifestyle. Thirteen-year-olds don't ponder the prospect that someday soon they'll have to give up all the amenities of the home life they enjoy with their parents. This is why we must let them know *at this age* that they should be ready to support themselves when they graduate from high school. Even if they take the four-year option of college and live at home, they'll be asked to make some major adjustments (see chapter 11).

High-school graduates who are willing to live in a furnished, rented room and use bus transportation to and from their job at a fast-food restaurant can leave home and support themselves at age seventeen or eighteen. Life will be grim, but if this is their choice, we must let them do it. I know of nothing that motivates young people to go on for further education more than the prospect of standing behind a fast-food counter the rest of their lives.

My wife, Fay, and I laid down the rule of leaving home for all four of our sons. Our oldest son, Steve, received an athletic scholarship and went away to college. Our second son, Dave, joined the army for the schooling it offered. Our third son, Pete, joined the navy for schooling. Our fourth son, Jonathan, took the four-year option and completed two years of college before he moved out with a sales job. All of the boys eventually married, and three have children. They all have good jobs and are doing quite well on their own.

Fay and I believe that it was our early training that prepared them for the difficult task of growing up and becoming independent adults. Age thirteen isn't too early to talk about leaving home and how to do it.

Another benefit of raising this issue as early as age thirteen is that children recognize from an early age that you want independence for them as much as they want it for themselves. I can't recall our kids ever telling me or my wife that we were standing in the way of their independence. As far as I know, they felt loved and secure in our home, but they knew that we were working for their independence as hard as they were.

Summer Work Although a thirteen-year-old's summer should be a free, unstructured time, we must let them know that when they turn fourteen, summers will be different. They will be spending more time working and saving money to buy things like sports equipment and the clothes they want. We will provide the basics, but if they want more expensive items, they will have to pay the difference. They also will be expected to save for their own recreational expenses, such as a fair share of things like a ski trip with the youth group at church.

By the time our sons were thirteen, they already had paper routes and did odd jobs like cutting grass and shoveling snow. So the idea of spending more of the summer hours working for pay wasn't difficult to implement when the time came. The important thing was getting them ready to start carrying more of their own weight financially by floating the idea at age thirteen.

Driver's License You may think that you have plenty of time to worry about your thirteen-year-old getting a driver's license. But that time will come all too quickly. You better say *now* what your expectations are. You may want to use the guidelines I suggest in chapter 10.

Dating Our children need to know that we have some expectations and rules about dating. They need to know that we're glad to see that they have interest in the opposite sex. But they'll not be permitted to date until they're age fifteen or sixteen. Their maturity at the time will determine when you actually permit them to go on a date. Until that time, group functions will be the way they cultivate opposite-sex relationships.

Thirteen-year-olds need to understand that you will not permit them to be with friends—either at the friends' houses or at your house—unless a responsible adult is present. This will raise the classic question, What's the matter, don't you trust me? The answer to that, which must be expressed in good humor, is, "Of course I don't trust you. I hope I raised you to be a red-blooded boy (or girl) who has a normal interest in the opposite sex and the desire to express that interest. I don't want to put you in a situation where that interest might get out of hand."

Too Early? I was talking with a group of parents at a seminar when one mother said, "Aren't you premature talking to *thirteen-year-olds* about these things? They're hardly out of childhood and are preoccupied with how they look and how to relate to the opposite sex, and you want us to talk with them about *leaving home?*"

I replied, "You're quite right. They're little more than children. And they're preoccupied with their appearance and the opposite sex. This is exactly the reason we need to talk to them about the demands the next four years will bring."

We lament the fact that adolescents are ill-prepared for adulthood and that we have twenty-four- and twenty-five-year-old kids still living at home, many of them behaving like irresponsible teenagers. The problem begins when our kids are thirteen. We treat them like children and don't prepare them for the realities of adolescence. Then, when they arrive at adolescence and it begins to dawn on them what adult independence and responsibility is about, they don't like what they see. They resist doing the hard work it takes to be independent and responsible.

And what do parents do? We either fume and fuss and fight with them about their irresponsible behavior, or we retreat into an angry silence and abandon the field of battle to them.

It's not premature to talk with thirteen-year-olds about these issues. If the developmental task for the thirteen-year-old is to get ready for the rigors of adolescence, then we better get on with the job of letting them know what's in store. We must help them think about their future realistically and understand that they can't have all the perks of home life *and* the independence of adolescence and adulthood.

It's tough parenting like this that pays off in grown children who have avoided the struggle of a protracted adolescence and are able to have pride in what *they* have accomplished. I can't tell you the joy it gives me to be with my adult sons and watch them function as responsible adults, husbands, and fathers. It is *their triumph*. Their mother and I couldn't do it for them.

Understanding Thirteen-Year-Olds' Behavior

Preparing thirteen-year-olds for the rigors of adolescence is a tough job because the mother's view I quoted above is correct: They are preoccupied with their appearance and how to relate to the opposite sex. That's a legitimate part of being thirteen, and we need to accept it in both our word and attitude of patience. Understanding some of the characteristics of this age will help us be more patient and understanding.

Uncommunicative and Inward Thirteen-year-olds' cognitive and emotional development opens new vistas that take time for them to ponder, understand, and absorb. As a result of this inner sorting-out process, they tend to be outwardly uncommunicative.

Thirteen-year-olds are reluctant to ask questions because they don't want to appear to be ignorant. If they do ask questions, give them simple, direct answers, *but don't pry*.

You may say, "Why do you ask?" to encourage further dialogue on the subject. But if they give a noncommittal answer such as, "I just wondered," drop it. Further attempts to discuss the subject will come across as prying and will make communication all the more difficult.

When they don't feel communicative, they sometimes withdraw to their room. They'll close the door, turn on music, and thumb through magazines. Don't worry about this behavior. They're doing the hard work of sorting things out.

When thirteen-year-olds withdraw during a family activity, parents sometimes wonder if they have offended their child. Don't take it personally. They just need to do some processing. They'll rejoin the family when they have sorted out as much as they can. Sometimes we get a clue to what has happened when they rejoin us and ask questions. Just answer the questions, but don't pry.

The uncommunicative thirteen-year-old often is touchy—quite a change from the good humor of the twelve-year-old. Avoid humor that comments on appearance or relationships, particularly boy-girl relationships. Though thirteen-year-olds may be critical of parents, peers, and siblings, they find it difficult to handle criticism of themselves, even that which is veiled in humor. Remember that self-image is a big issue with them. Looking good to their peers is very important.

Sometimes parents react to their children's need to look good by "keeping them humble," being critical of their appearance or primping. They don't need to be kept humble by parents or siblings. They put themselves down too much as it is. When they primp in front of the mirror—and boys can primp as much as girls—and joke about being "gorgeous" or a "hunk," go along with them and reinforce it. Say something like, "Watch out Eisenhower Junior High!"

Respect Privacy and Confidentiality Thirteen-year-olds need privacy. Their room is off-limits to everyone. And they expect to be able to have phone conversations where they can't be overheard.

Parents sometimes get nervous about secrecy, particularly when their daughter spends hours on the phone talking to girlfriends in hushed tones. Parents want to know what the secrecy is about.

Well, if you must know, it's mainly about the opposite sex, and sometimes it's about grades and teachers and what's going on in the lives of their friends. One of the ways your daughter finds out that she thinks and acts like her peers is to have these lengthy conversations.

Boys don't seem to have this need. Gender difference emerges here. Girls have a need to have close confidential relationships that explore the social intricacies of what's going on and why. Boys get together to do things. And as they grow older, we see a refinement in this divergence. To boys, a peer's performance, whether it be on the athletic field or in that person's ability to be mischievous, is what's important. To girls, liking is directly related to acceptance or rejection. As a consequence, boys hone their athletic (or performance-oriented) skills, while girls concentrate on their social skills. This tends to widen the gap between boys and girls of the same age, with girls being far more socially skilled and able to outwit boys.

Respect your child's need for privacy. But make it absolutely clear to them that the privacy of their room or the phone *will not* be respected if you have reason to believe that something may be harmful or dangerous to them.

Let them know that you'll give them fair warning when you intend to invade their privacy, like shaking down their room or listening to conversations. For example, you may say, "Something's going on that concerns me. You have been exceptionally secretive and troubled [or whatever the behavior], and it's my responsibility to make sure that you arrive at adulthood physically and emotionally intact. If something's going on that I should know about, I want you to tell me before I find out for myself."

This will give you the freedom to find out what's going on. But be reluctant to exercise that right. Talk to other parents, your pastor, or a professional counselor to see if you're overreacting.

Kids have a way of letting adults know indirectly that they want us to know about something that's going on.

Sometimes it's a leak from a friend or a sibling that your child is involved with alcohol or drugs. Other times, our children will make their behavior obvious so we'll step in.

When one of our sons was in junior high, he left a marijuana pipe on the nightstand in his bedroom. When I asked him about it, he confessed that he had experimented with marijuana. This led to a constructive discussion about drug use and our expectations of him.

Girls, and their use of the phone, raises a practical question. Should they be granted unlimited, private use? No. The rest of the family has a right to receive incoming calls and make calls of their own without the thirteen-year-old tying it up. If she wants to make a call to exchange information, she should be limited to five minutes. But the family phone is not to be used for visiting with friends.

What will you do if she asks for a separate phone line? That may be a possibility, with adequate rules and restrictions. Rather than suggest a plan of action, let me suggest some questions you can ask when you make agreements with your teenagers.

1. Is this thirteen-year-old responsible enough to pay for his or her share of the cost and abide by conditions laid down by parents? Has he or she already shown responsibility and a willingness to go along with conditions? For example, are chores done without constant reminders? Is your teenager pretty good about obeying the rules about activities, friends, and curfew? If the answer is yes, the agreement you work out probably will be honored.

2. Is your teenager mature enough to understand that you are asking him or her to carry a substantial share of the cost because you want to teach financial responsibility? If the answer is yes, having a phone probably will be a good learning experience.

3. Are you the kind of tough parent who will insist that the agreement be honored if your teenager fails to hold up

his or her part from time to time? What's your record in firmly and consistently insisting that your kids obey rules?

For example, you have agreed that your daughter will pay her monthly phone bill when due. If she doesn't, you'll unplug the phone and remove it until she does. Are you willing to do that? If the answer is yes, then you probably have an agreement you can handle. Tough parenting follows through on agreements, and one like this isn't especially difficult to implement when your teenager knows that the phone company stops service to adults who don't pay their bill. Kids learn adult responsibility when we insist that they abide by adult rules.

4. Is the agreement simple? The test is your ability to put it in writing. If you find that making the agreement clear and workable requires you to add many explanations and conditions, it's probably not simple and free of hassles.

For example, your daughter wants to pay for the phone by bartering services such as extra baby-sitting for her little brother. Be careful. You can agree to provide enough extra work so she can pay her share, but you have no guarantee that she'll take advantage of the opportunities. It's far better for you to let her know verbally that you'll give her opportunities to earn enough money for her share of the phone. But it's *her* responsibility to have the money when her bill comes due. You give no credit and take no promises about future work.

Your agreement would simply state that she is responsible to pay the bill when it's due and that phone service will be interrupted after a certain number of days from the due date. You don't have to keep reminding her that she hasn't taken advantage of opportunities to earn money and that she has a bill coming due. If she is unprepared to pay her bill, then she has to give up her phone until she does. This takes tough parenting.

When you have put your agreement in writing, give your teenager a copy in a manila folder labeled "phone agreement." Some parents sign the agreement and have the teenager do it too. I never found this necessary and have felt it a little too formal. I've never had my kids question the validity of an unsigned agreement.

Use this opportunity to get your teenagers started making a file of important papers. If they don't have a file drawer available, go to an office-supply store and buy a cardboard file box and a supply of folders. As their file grows, you can show them how to break down the material by subject matter so they can retrieve it easily.

This kind of written agreement may seem like a lot of work, and it is. But it's part of parental responsibility to teach our children how to live in a world of adult privilege and responsibility.

Sexual Development

At least three issues are important here: boy-girl relationships, father-daughter relationships, and sexual aberrations such as homosexuality, exhibitionism, and peeping.

Boy-Girl Relationships Our children need to believe that their sexual development is normal because it's part of the larger concern of self-image. They need to know that they're like their peers in this area.

Let's give them a break here. Let their concern about their sexual development be between themselves and their peers or perhaps with a trusted adult like a youth pastor or a teacher in a sex-education class. I don't think you or I would have been comfortable with going to either of our parents with questions and doubts about our sexual development or what we could do to enhance attraction from the opposite sex. If we have been accessible as parents, they know they can come to us with concerns like this if they want to. But their need to keep sexual matters private usually makes them turn elsewhere.

Father-Daughter Relationships As children grow away from their mother, their father becomes more important. This is especially true of the father-daughter relationship.

Though sons need to have their masculinity validated by their fathers, their relationship is charged with fewer sexual implications than the father-daughter relationship. Sons need to know that their fathers think they are becoming well-developed men, physically and sexually. But daughters' way of validating their femininity has no parallel between sons and mothers. Daughters often look to their fathers for evidences that they are sexually desirable.

For example, daughters often will be coquettish or provocative with their fathers as a way of asking, "Do you think I'm a sexually attractive female?" The father has a double responsibility in how he replies. On one hand, he should answer his daughter's questions with a resounding yes! On the other hand, he must make it clear that his affirmation of her sex appeal is pure and fatherly, and that his sexual loyalty remains exclusively with her mother.

It's important that a father doesn't respond to this behavior negatively or chide his daughter for her behavior. He can back off from her sexually charged behavior and say something like, "Honey, I can't hold you in my lap any more because you're not a little girl. You're turning out to be a very attractive woman." This will do worlds for her self-image.

A mother's response is important too. Rather than get angry about your daughter's behavior, talk to your husband about it and let him handle it. And be tolerant of your daughter's competitive behavior. She may even have fantasies of replacing you in her daddy's affections. If your husband handles it well, you won't have to do anything.

Sexual Aberrations

1. *Pornography and peeping.* Boys at this age are extremely curious about the female body. They may resort to looking at "adult" magazines at the drugstore or peeking in someone's window while a woman is dressing.

Age thirteen is a good time to say something about how pornography degrades both women and men. You don't have to give a special lecture on the subject. Just take advantage of the opportunity to say something when the subject comes up.

Though pornography should be discouraged, our boys will still satisfy this urge in their imagination. Peeping is more serious because it involves a violation of the law. Look for opportunities to open this subject with your son and address the legal consequences of the behavior while granting that curiosity about the female body is perfectly understandable. We don't want to discourage interest in the opposite sex in either our sons or daughters.

2. *Exhibitionism and homosexuality.* Thirteen-year-olds who are dealing with their sexuality sometimes grapple with the problems of exhibitionism and homosexuality. Be aware that it's often at this age we become aware of the likelihood of exhibitionism in boys and homosexuality in both boys and girls. I deal with the issue of homosexuality more thoroughly in chapter 12.

Illegal exhibitionism often is the result of uncertainty about one's sexual identity. It's a way of saying, "See, I'm a male." Separate the need for your child to be sure of his male identity from the legal complications of his behavior. If you should find out what's going on, say, "I think I understand how you feel. But doing that is sure to result in a complaint to the police."

Although female exhibitionism usually isn't illegal, it is an area of concern for parents to see their thirteen-year-old daughter dress and behave provocatively and inappropriately. You may find it helpful to view her behavior as uncertainty of her acceptance as a female rather than a disgusting attempt to seduce males. But she does need to know that certain women's clothing styles may arouse men and that as Christians we are called to modesty in our dress.

I mention homosexuality, but I don't feel it's as pervasive a problem as the media would suggest. But for those who wrestle with it, homosexuality is very painful for the whole family.

This is a subject that your child isn't going to discuss with you. You may have some doubts about your child's gender identity and sexual interest, but parents often don't find out about homosexuality until sometime in their child's late teens or early adulthood. Parents who are concerned about the possibility of their child's homosexual orientation should consult the resource page at the end of the book for organizations that can help.

Summary

Thirteen-year-olds may think they're ready for independence and adulthood. But the reality is, they are just preparing for adolescence. We can help them prepare for it by talking about what's ahead. In four or five years they'll be leaving home. What are their thoughts? Do they know what we expect of them when they graduate from high school? They need to know that we expect them to start learning financial responsibility by working summers and saving to meet some of their wants and needs. They need to know when they can expect to date and what rules go with the privilege. They need to know that when they get a driver's license, they'll have to abide by restrictions and conditions.

What we are doing with our thirteen-year-old is explaining the game of adolescence and how to play it. It's also a game with rules. If we consistently apply them and our teenagers abide by them, it can be a great time for both parents and teenagers.

10

Helping Them Become Adults: Ages Fourteen Through Seventeen

Janet hung around after the parenting seminar, obviously wanting to talk to me, but she waited until everyone had left before she approached. When she spoke, she choked back the tears and said, "I wish I had known all this a few years ago."

I had just spoken about helping teenagers become adults, and my emphasis was on why they behave so badly toward their parents. Something had moved this mother to tears.

"My daughter doesn't live with me any more," she continued. "She lives with her father, whom I divorced years ago. I've always had difficulty getting along with her because she reminds me so much of him—the selfishness and self-centeredness. By the time she was sixteen years old, I had had it with her and all her threats that she was going to move out.

"Now I understand what she was going through. She wasn't deliberately being ugly to me. She was just trying to get her distance so she could grow up, and I took it personally."

Janet is like many parents of teenagers I talk to. They find it very difficult to handle their teenagers' behavior because sometimes it seems so self-centered. They don't seem to have any appreciation for the feelings of parents or anyone else in the family. For Janet, understanding what was going on in Cindy made a big difference.

In the last chapter we saw that age thirteen was a time to get ready. Age fourteen signals the beginning of adolescence, when teenagers face three daunting tasks: developing healthy opposite-sex relationships, deciding on vocational direction, and gaining emancipation from their parents. Though complete emancipation from parents doesn't come until they leave home and are self-supporting, age fourteen is the time to lay the groundwork.

Three Developmental Tasks

With the three tasks in mind, let's look at how we can help our teenagers become adults, especially without taking personally their alienating behavior.

Healthy Opposite-Sex Relationships Parents may be a little uneasy about helping their teenagers establish opposite-sex relationships. A mother I talked to at a parenting seminar expressed her fear: "My daughter's already so boy-crazy that I worry about her!"

By "healthy opposite-sex relationships," I'm not referring to sexual interest. Given the normal development of our children, a strong sexual interest is the easy part. The hard part for a parent is helping them grasp the difference between sex and intimacy. Parents must understand three things if we are to do this job well.

1. *Loss of parent-child intimacy.* Opposite-sex relationships are important because teenagers need to compensate for the *loss of intimacy with parents.* Parents and children have shared experiences, affirmation, understanding, and unselfish love. When teenagers move toward independence, they also look to other people to fill those needs for intimacy.

2. *The nature of true intimacy.* Intimacy is not the same as sexual intercourse. One can have sexual intercourse without intimacy. Sexual intercourse is a married couple's *celebration* and *outward expression* of their emotional intimacy.

What we want to encourage in our teenagers at this stage is *nonsexual* intimacy of empathy and affection. Empathy does more than understand the other person's feelings; empathy feels the other person's feelings—both positive and negative ones—and cares enough to be there with the other person. It establishes a profound bond.

Affection is nonsexual caring, such as nonsexual touching or a kiss on the cheek. It's the kind of caring that a parent shows a child and says, "You're nice to be with."

3. *The failure of sex education.* Given the true nature of intimacy and the need teenagers have to establish it with the opposite sex, we can see why much sex education today is a failure. Sex education that focuses primarily on sexual intercourse and reproduction fails to educate our teenagers in the true nature of a love relationship and fails to recognize teenagers' need to replace what they're losing in child-parent intimacy with an intimate relationship to someone else. I believe that our teenagers need information about the physical aspects of an opposite-sex relationship. But let's not confuse this with intimacy as manifested by empathy and affection. Our teenagers need to know

that they can be, and should be, intimate without express-
ing it in sexual ways.

I don't believe for a minute that proper education in
emotional intimacy alone is going to prevent sexual
intercourse among unmarried teenagers. But it's a start. I
see the need for further education in heading off sexual
activity in teenagers.

First of all, much sexual intercourse in the teen years
isn't planned but happens when they put themselves in a
compromising situation and things get out of hand. By
compromising situation I mean the couple finds themselves in a place—a home while parents are out or a car in
an out-of-the-way place—where they can have sexual
activity without fear of anyone discovering them. Teenagers need to know that if they don't intend to have sexual
intercourse, they must stay away from compromising
situations.

Second, teenagers need to understand that they have an
unrealistic sense of invincibility. They believe that nothing
bad is going to happen to them. They are sure that they
can have intercourse without protection and nothing will
happen.

On one hand this is a very positive feature of teenage
psychology. In order to face the rigors and uncertainties of
adulthood, they must believe that nothing bad is going to
happen to them. It's *good* to feel invincible in facing the
future. But it's bad when they do dangerous things as a
result.

Third, I believe that much sexual activity occurs in
teenagers who have been emotionally starved by their
parents. Remember that teenagers are looking for someone to replace the lost intimacy with parents. But what
happens when a girl *never had* intimacy with her parents?
And what happens when, hoping for intimacy through a
sexual relationship with her boyfriend, she gets only sex? A

child of her own to love and love her could offer the *hope* of intimacy she never got from her parents or boyfriend. The reality, of course, is quite different from the hope.

We do know that in low-income families, teenage girls often find a measure of self-worth in giving birth to a child.[1] The need to love and be loved with genuine intimacy, the kind that a mother and child experience, is fundamental. And if teenagers didn't experience this kind of love and intimacy from their own parents, they'll look for it in sex and possibly in pregnancy.

If we are to help our teenagers with the task of establishing a healthy opposite-sex relationship, we must educate our teenagers about four areas:

1. Make sure your teenagers know the difference between sex and intimacy.

2. Make sure your teenagers have adequate information about sexual reproduction and pregnancy prevention. This includes knowing that none of the methods of birth control is foolproof.

3. Help keep them from harm's way by vetoing any activity that may lead to a sexually compromising situation, such as being together at home when you're away or going on unsupervised trips with other couples.

4. Explain to them the phenomenon of teenage invincibility. Express your affirmation in their courage to face the future without fear, but help them see that a feeling of invincibility could lead them to do unwise things.

Vocational Direction If we do a good job introducing thirteen-year-olds to what we expect over the next four or five years and if we continue to reinforce it in our conversations, their concern over vocation will surface from time to time. It often will take the form of worrying that they don't know what they want to do to support themselves.

We need to assure them that lots of people don't automatically *choose* their vocations. It's something they grow into as they become more aware of themselves, their interests, and their aptitudes. As teenagers face various opportunities, they will find where they fit. Many adults are in careers they hadn't dreamed of considering, but when opportunities came their way, they took them. With the rapid expansion of technology and services, our teenagers may find work in vocations *that don't even exist today*.

It's important for teenagers to get a good basic education beyond high school, whether that education is academic or vocational. If they choose a liberal-arts program, they shouldn't view their education as training for a particular job. Undergraduate education teaches them how to function as competent adults who can read, write, communicate, and do basic math effectively. Education in the basics will enable them to take advantage of a variety of job opportunities as they grow older and focus their interests.

Vocational testing that includes intelligence, interest, aptitude, and personality testing can benefit teenagers. They can see how their interests match their aptitude and intelligence in that area. A teenager may have a particular interest but not the intelligence, aptitude, and personality to do a certain job. The testing can save that person the frustration of being in a job that isn't a good fit.

Sometimes a person has the intelligence, aptitude, and personality for certain work, but not the interest. That was true in my case. When I was a teenager, I took a battery of tests that showed I had what it took to be a teacher, writer, or minister—three things I had absolutely no interest in. At the time, my two buddies, Ted and Bill, and I were preparing ourselves for work in salvage diving, especially for sunken treasure. We planned to save our money and go to a vocational diving school in California to learn the trade.

Then, at age seventeen, I became a Christian. I still wanted to go to diving school so I joined the Air Force to save money for my diving training. But God had other plans. My love for him and my interest in serving him grew to the point that I decided to go into the ministry. When I got out of the Air Force, I went to college and seminary and into the ministry, which included some college teaching and writing. Now, having experienced all three areas confirmed by my earlier vocational testing, I'm involved in a marriage and family ministry that includes all three skills—teaching, writing, ministry.

The point is, vocation is more serendipitous than we sometimes think. Accidental discoveries that send us in new directions often are accidental discoveries about *ourselves*. Our third son, Pete, who at seventeen had very little grasp of his skills or the kind of life he wanted to pursue, joined the Navy to find himself and his vocation. Ten years later he was a chief petty officer and technical instructor in metallurgy and nuclear propulsion systems, feeling happy and fulfilled.

A major impediment to our kids' finding themselves vocationally is a lack of tough parenting. When our teenagers know that they are expected to get out and support themselves after high school, vocational school, or college, they'll examine their own interests and goals with greater seriousness. Parents who send the message, "You may stay at home until you find yourself," give their teenagers little reason to do so. Knowing they better be ready to support themselves has a way of enlivening vocational concerns.

Cultivate their desire to explore interests by stimulating two developmental strengths: feelings of invincibility (they're ready to take on the world) and the need for independence from their parents. Talk in positive terms about their growing independence. Rather than lament the difficulty teenagers have making it on their own, explore possibilities that will lead toward independence.

Some teenagers, both boys and girls, find military service an attractive option. The merchant marine, though a tough life with rough people, may be the ticket for a mature young person looking for adventure.

Sometimes extended family or close friends in another state are willing to take teenagers as boarders if they are willing to work a full-time job and help with the chores. I've told my sons that my wife and I are willing to do this for our grandchildren if the time comes that they're not ready for further education beyond high school and need a fresh look at life. Teenagers often will cooperate with other adults in ways they won't with their own parents.

An entirely new environment sometimes opens possibilities that teenagers can't see while they're living at home. Though teenagers may be doing the same kind of menial work and chores they would have done at home, new experiences and new friends open new possibilities. Remember that we're trying to help our teenagers get a fresh look at themselves and their opportunities in life. For high-school graduates who didn't want further education, new experiences may even make them decide to go back to school.

The question of vocation is more compelling now than it ever has been for girls. Even if a girl marries, she probably will be expected to work outside the home. What does she want in life? Women who would like to "have it all"—career, marriage, and children—are finding that it's difficult to do.

It's not so difficult for a man to "have it all" because old patterns of marriage and family still hang on. Though men are taking on more responsibility for home and family, the truly egalitarian marriage is more fiction than fact. The husband/father is usually the primary wage earner, and the wife/mother usually remains the primary caregiver.

The old division of labor with a go-to-work husband and a stay-at-home wife and mother is finding more and more appeal to women today. Sometimes the husband is the stay-at-home parent, but women often feel they're losing something in not being the primary caregiver.

The teenage girl considering what she wants out of life has more to think about than vocation. If she can't have it all, then what does she want?

Emancipation The third major task teenagers face is emancipation from parents. This freedom is both emotional and physical. Their emotional emancipation happens, as we have seen, as their need for intimacy transfers from parents to boyfriends or girlfriends. Physical separation should begin in two areas: their day-to-day needs and financial dependency.

1. *Less day-to-day dependency.* By the time our children are adolescents, we should expect them to be taking care of more of their everyday needs on their own.

One mother complained to me that she had the hardest time getting her daughter out of bed in the morning. And when she did get up, she was grouchy and often missed the bus to school and made her mother take her. It was a constant source of friction between them.

I asked the mother, "What would happen if you gave your daughter the responsibility to get herself up and to school, bus or no bus?"

She replied, "Claudia would never make it."

"And what would happen if you let that be Claudia's problem?"

"Claudia probably wouldn't go to school."

I asked her, "What would happen if you grounded Claudia for not going to school?"

"She would create a terrible scene."

"How?"

"She'd rant and rave and probably disobey me."

"Then what would happen?"

"She'd probably get away with it."

"It sounds like Claudia is tougher than her mother. Is that the message you want to send her?"

"No. But what do I do?"

"Get tough. Let her know that she is responsible to get herself up in the morning, and if she misses the bus, she walks to school. And if she doesn't go to school, she's grounded. And if she violates grounding, then you better be ready to start lifting other privileges."

"Like what?"

"Phone privileges. The use of her stereo and television."

"But she'll tell me that I can't do that. The stereo and television were gifts to her."

"Tell her that she can use *her* stereo and television, but not with *your* electricity."

Claudia's mother needed to practice tough parenting. She took courage from knowing that Claudia would see that her mom was willing to do whatever it took to get the desired results.

That's what tough parenting is all about. One reason many parents don't practice tough parenting is that they dread the confrontation and conflict it often produces in teenagers. Both parents must work together, or the teenager will divide and conquer. If you are a single parent, get support from a close friend or from a counselor. Most of my work with parents and teenagers is with the parents. When I can get parents to work together and teach them to handle confrontation without caving in or engaging in counter-hysterics, more often than not the teenager cooperates. If you've lost control of your household, get professional help.

2. *Less financial dependency.* By age fourteen, teenagers ought to be carrying more financial responsibility. They should know that they'll get a few dollars allowance a week to spend as they wish. But when it comes to big-ticket items like designer clothes and ski trips, they need to know that they'll have to contribute financially.

What their contribution should be depends on what they want and how much you're willing to contribute. A helpful principle is this: They must work as hard for what they want as you do. If they know that you're on a tight budget and that your money is already allocated to things that benefit them (food, room and furnishings, transportation, fees for activities, etc.), they may be more cooperative in contributing. They need to learn that things don't come free; it takes work—their work.

Though fourteen-year-olds may not be able to get a regular job and paycheck, they can find many money-making opportunities. Yard work, baby-sitting, and paper routes are good jobs for beginners. Don't be sexist in the choice of jobs. Our sons have done baby-sitting, and girls are more than capable of doing yard work and paper routes.

If you're financially able, you can put them to work for you in the yard or house for minimum wage. Although this arrangement helps the teenager earn money, it may not be worth it if the situation results in emotional flareups or further stress on the parent-child relationship. Ideally, they should begin at this age to work for other people, learning to be accountable to meeting other people's expectations of them, learning to earn money in ways that are independent from their parents.

Let them know that if they can't come up with their share of the money, they'll have to do without. If they want it badly enough, they'll find work. Unless, of course, they have found they can manipulate their parents into giving them everything they want on a silver platter.

At age sixteen, our kids should be able to work all day Saturday at a regular job and have at least a twenty-hour-a-week, if not a full-time, summer job. They may complain that Saturday and summer is vacation time. Let them know that this is part of the price of growing up and gaining independence. Tell them that this is just the beginning. The older they get, the less free time they'll have at their disposal.

Parents sometimes object that it is an unnecessary burden to expect good students or athletes to work, particularly when the kids can parlay their hard work into an academic or athletic scholarship. The point is worth considering, but only on a case-by-case basis. One problem with this thinking is that good students and athletes often aren't really working that hard at it. It's easy. Or they tend to become prima donnas. They don't have to work like other kids because they're special. We rob them of the opportunity to do the tough work of character development that comes with having to carry more of their own responsibility.

Tough parenting that's determined to make our kids less physically dependent on us really isn't that difficult. Most of the time, we don't have to do a lot other than avoid caving in to our kids' demands. But for some parents, that's the tough part.

Age Characteristics

Not all teenagers are alike. Their behavior changes as they move from age fourteen through age seventeen.

Age Fourteen Age fourteen is a more agreeable time than age thirteen. Fourteen-year-olds are more outgoing, less touchy, and more secure in who they are. Friendship and socialization are important. Though you may feel jealous of their opportunities to go places and do things with their friends, it may help to remember that they're doing the hard work of being fourteen-year-olds.

Boys and girls show considerable difference in their physical development. Fourteen-year-old boys look immature, though they experience rapid growth in height. They're interested in girls, but they're less obvious about opposite-sex interest than girls.

By this age, most girls are menstruating, and they have almost achieved their adult height. Their pubic hair is full grown, and their breasts are approaching full maturity. Girls who are exceptionally mature or slow in development or obese may find gym class an embarrassing experience. They don't want the other girls to see them changing clothes or showering. If your daughter has this problem, talk to her gym teacher about it privately during a regular parent-teacher conference.

Fourteen-year-olds can be disagreeable and angry when their younger siblings bug them or get into their room. Let them know that you understand their anger, but they're not to act it out by yelling or hitting. When you hear a confrontation coming, separate the children. The invasion of your teenager's room might be prevented with a lock on the door. It should be understood, however, that parents should have a key.

Emotions run deep at this age, so expect tears from time to time, even from boys. It's extremely important that dads don't ridicule their son's tears. Your son needs to know that it's okay for boys and men to cry.

The dating issue will come up again, particularly from your daughter. If she is immature, you may need to let her know that she'll have to wait until she's sixteen, unless she is particularly mature and responsible in choosing suitable friends.

Age fourteen is a good time to talk about a daughter's growing away from parents and the need to establish intimacy with a boy. She needs to know that boys and girls feel differently about attraction to each other. Girls are more interested in tender feelings and probably are looking for more authentic intimacy than boys are. Boys tend to confuse sexual feelings with intimacy and think that kissing and petting are the same as intimacy.

Girls are able to distinguish between their sexual needs and an emotional need to be close. But because boys don't make that distinction, girls often permit sexual advances because that's what boys want and that's how girls are able to get closeness.

Girls need to know that they don't have to be sexual to get close. And boys need to know that they should learn to respect this difference in girls.

Age Fifteen Age fifteen is a very difficult time. Though fifteen-year-olds don't cognitively understand what's going on with the loss of child-parent intimacy, nature encourages them to create more distance and be less dependent on parents for their emotional needs.

They create distance in ways that parents often find difficult to handle. They act hardboiled and indifferent to the sensitivities of parents and siblings. Their I-don't-care attitude touches everything of value to us: family life, church, education, and their future.

At all stages of child development, *negative identity* comes before *positive identity*. Kids know what they *don't* want (which usually is what we want), but they haven't yet matured sufficiently to know what they *do* want.

Our parenting should be up-front but as unobtrusive as possible. This doesn't mean we take a see-no-evil attitude and let our teenagers do as they please. They need to know that we want their independence as much as they do, but as long as they're minors, parents are responsible before the law to have their children under control. Because of this we must set and enforce reasonable rules.

1. Rules. Fifteen-year-olds would like to come and go as they please with no restrictions or accountability. If you already have established rules about friendships and activities, it's just a matter of enforcing those rules.

Curfew is important. Fifteen-year-olds should not be out socializing on school nights, unless it's a special activity with parental approval. But those events should be the exception rather than the rule.

Your teenager should be home after school or school activities. In general, any socializing that takes place should be from after school till supper. We may want to make exceptions to this rule, but identify them as special cases. If you have no family supper together or no set time that you eat on weekday evenings, set a time for your teenager to be home. Six o'clock is liberal enough.

Your teenager should know that weekday evenings are for homework. If they say they have no homework, let them know that they'll be expected to read during the time set for study—with no television. Background music may be permitted. They may read the newspaper, magazines, or books. What we are after here is the improvement of their minds, which unlimited television viewing doesn't help. You may want to make an exception to the television rule if your teenager wants to watch something educational such as programs aired on the Public Broadcasting Service.

A liberal bedtime for fifteen-year-olds is ten o'clock. Some kids may need to turn in earlier, especially if they must get up early for school. Expect them to be in bed, with no television. A quiet radio may be permitted if it facilitates sleep.

A later curfew on Friday and Saturday is appropriate. Eleven o'clock is reasonable enough for a mature fifteen-year-old. If your teenagers resist this decision, be open to negotiation but make it clear that responsible parenting means that you will not be going to bed until they come home. You need to be accessible to them or any others who need to contact you when they are out.

If your teenagers argue that you don't need to stay up for them, they need to know you're not staying up for them; you're staying up because you're responsible to see that they make curfew and that they have had no problems. If teenagers know that parents will be up when they get home and they must run the parent "gauntlet," they'll most likely observe curfew and not come home with alcohol on their breath.

Don't let your teenagers come home and go directly to their room without talking to you. If they do, knock on their door and ask them if their evening went well. You'll be able to tell if everything's all right by the way they behave. Fifteen-year-olds are poor liars.

A major problem you may have with your fifteen-year-old is disinterest in church. If your child is not willing to go to the morning worship as a family activity, do insist that he or she participate in church youth functions.

If your church doesn't have an adequate youth program, you may need to find one that does in order to get your teenager involved. Another possibility is to allow participation in another church's youth program without moving the whole family to a new church.

High schools often have Campus Life or Young Life programs. These can make a major contribution to teenagers' spiritual and social lives.

If you live in a rural area that doesn't offer a lot of activities for your teenagers, get together with other parents and establish something for them yourselves. It need not be a formal program. Supervised activities such as skating, bowling, hiking, camping, or boating will give them fun times together. You may include a Bible devotional with the activity.

2. *Enforcing rules*. Enforcing rules for fifteen-year-olds takes finesse. Above all, don't get involved in a game of Uproar. Teenagers are great at distracting us by creating an uproar—starting a family fight by provoking us to anger.

We also must not be naïve about granting permission. Though most of our teenagers will obey rules if gently nudged to do so, we must be realistic. Some parents find that when their teenagers ask for permission to do something or go somewhere, they ask in a way that is designed to get permission. They aren't committed to telling the truth, the whole truth, and nothing but the truth.

For example, your daughter wants to go cruising around town with some girlfriends and older boys. She suspects the guys will bring beer, because they've done it before. But she won't tell you what she really wants to do.

Instead, she'll tell you that she wants to go to Lori's house, and that's the truth—at least part of it. Lori is an approved friend, and she says that Lori's mother will be home. But what she doesn't tell you is that she and Lori are going to try to get Lori's mother to give them permission to go to Tina's house where the guys are going to pick them up. Tina isn't an approved friend.

You know that this has happened before, and even though Lori's mother does her best to keep the girls in line, you believe it may happen again.

What do you do? One possibility is not to permit your daughter to go to Lori's house because you don't think her mother can handle the girls. Another possibility is to let her go to Lori's house, but let her know that you're going to be checking up to see that she's there.

Here's where we can expect tough parenting to be tested. Your daughter will ask, "Don't you trust me?"

You can reply, "I don't know how to answer that except to say that trustworthiness begets trust. You've disappointed me before, so all I can say now is that evidence of your trustworthiness will do worlds for my trust."

If you do give permission, make it clear that your permission is based on the agreed-on activities; if any change is made, you need to discuss it and decide whether or not you will grant permission for the new plans. This will keep her from using the alibi that they suddenly decided to do something else.

When you do call her at Lori's, don't do it just once; call at least twice. All you need say is, "Hi, just checking in. I'm at home if you need me."

Enforcing rules requires that parents work together. Your teenager may get a no from one parent and then go to the other parent for permission. As a rule, consult the other parent, particularly when things sound fishy. The other parent may have additional information that will affect the decision.

Age Sixteen

Age sixteen is a good stage. Teenagers begin to feel that they'll make it as independent adults. Because teenagers begin driving and dating at age sixteen, they need some clear guidelines about these activities.

1. *Driving*. Driving is a *privilege*, not a right. It's a privilege that may be lifted by law or by parents, if they see a need to do so.

In most families the car is shared, which means that the teenager will not have unrestricted use. It's unwise to give teenagers a set of keys to the family car because it suggests more access than you intend. If they have to get the keys every time they use the car, it will give you more control.

Restrict your teenagers not only on the amount they use the car but also where they go and who their passengers are. This will discourage them from using the car to cruise with their friends.

If they expect to be included on the family auto-insurance policy, they should be required to pay the difference in the increased premium. If they want to know how much that will be, give them the phone number of your insurance agent and have them find out. If they're too timid to make the call, don't do it for them. You can help them ask the right questions and even rehearse what they're going to say. But making the call is part of growing up.

Even if you have the money to pay the increase of premium, don't do it. It only fosters dependence, robs them of a realistic view of what it costs to operate a car, and delays their maturity. Our teenagers don't suddenly assume their own financial responsibility. They gradually are introduced to it, and this is one way to do it.

Be prepared to restrict your teenager's use of the car if he or she breaks any driving rules you have set up. How much to restrict depends on the seriousness of the violation.

Teenagers also should buy their own gas. The question is, How do you determine how much they should contribute? Someone may suggest checking the mileage before and after they use the car and charge a per-mile fee. But more often than not, you'll forget to do it. Others may suggest having their teenagers contribute a certain amount of money for gas each week. But how do we determine an equitable amount?

As the father of four teenage sons and two foster daughters, I've found it difficult to come up with a solution they can't beat—except one. And this solution is based on the principle I talked about in the last chapter with regard to having a private phone. *Make your rule on the gas simple and hassle free.*

The agreement is this: everyone buys his or her own gas for the car. In order to make this work, you must *never fill the tank* unless you're going on a trip. Buy just enough gas to run your errands so when your teenagers get in the car, *they* are confronted with not having enough gas to get where they want. They'll try to avoid buying gas and run on empty. When they call and say they have run out of gas, tell them it's their responsibility to get gas and get home. If you must bail them out, slap a car restriction on them. But never, never, buy a full tank of gas.

The agreement is hassle free: you never have to remind them to buy gas. If they want to get where they're going, they have no other choice.

Though it may seem like a lot of unnecessary work to buy your gas this way, I've found this plan much simpler and easier to manage than anything else I've tried.

2. Dating. When your teenagers start to date, discuss your expectations with them, setting down some clear guidelines. Tell them you'll want to know who they're dating and where they're going. If it's a first date, you may not know the person and may have to go along with it unless you have good reason not to. But if your teenager begins to date this person regularly, you can get acquainted by including him or her in family functions. If you honestly believe this person is a bad influence or this person won't associate with the family, exercise your veto power. If your teenager insists on seeing this person behind your back, you have a matter that is getting out of hand. I'll discuss this more fully in chapter 12.

Your daughter probably will want to date older boys. Though this is expected because teenage boys are developmentally behind girls of the same age, it's generally not wise, particularly if the boys are two or more years older than the girl. However, you must deal with this on a case-by-case basis. An older boy *might* be a very stabilizing influence on your daughter.

Age Seventeen

Age seventeen is a mixed bag. In school your seventeen-year-old is a junior or senior, socially at the head of the school or almost there.

Seventeen-year-olds' major concern is what to do after graduation. Having prepared your teenagers with the rules of education beyond high school and having reinforced them along the way, you'll find it easier to review your expectations again: They go to college, vocational school, or are prepared to make it on their own.

Teenagers experience great consternation over these options because they don't know what they want to do. Vocational guidance certainly is in order. But they still must make a decision for now.

If they decide on vocational school or college, check out the school of choice, particularly if it's a vocational school. Some vocational schools make big promises but don't deliver. This also is true of some secretarial schools.

Expect your teenagers to contribute to their education. You must feel they're working as hard to get their education as you are. To do less is to coddle them and keep them from facing the economic reality that education is expensive.

This is another step in helping them gain independence. They have a naïve idea about practical economics. It seems so easy for their parents; it ought to be that easy for them. But they don't realize that we are twenty to thirty years ahead of them in earning power and wisdom.

Some parents have difficulty putting pressure on their teenagers to carry their share financially, particularly if the parents are able to pay their teenagers' way. You do them no favor by doing what they should do for themselves. Be tough. Make them carry their share.

In these times, economic emancipation is perhaps the most elusive goal. We see too many developmentally arrested, emotionally immature people who haven't been forced, through tough parenting, to carry their share of the load. Our children are not truly free from us until they are financially independent.

Summary

As parents of teenagers we have three major tasks: first, to help our teenagers establish a healthy relationship with the opposite sex; second, to help them set their vocational goals so that they'll be able to support themselves; third, to help them achieve their freedom.

You can achieve these tasks by remembering that tough parenting really is loving parenting. Parents who love their kids permit them to go through the struggle for independence. And when they emerge as self-confident adults, it will be *their* achievement, and they'll thank you for letting them do it.

11

Leaving Home: Age Eighteen to Young Adulthood

Well, you've almost made it. Your teenager is nearly an adult. Your tough parenting efforts are about to pay off in adult children who are prepared for independence.

Though we hear at every hand how tough it is for young adults to live away from home, by 1988, forty-six percent of adults between the ages of eighteen to twenty-four were living on their own.[1] Many American parents can be proud of the fact that they have done a good job of preparing their children for adult independence.

A major reason for this is tough parenting. Parents of grown children who are making it on their own have helped their children understand the importance of education. They didn't just *tell* their kids that they need an education. They introduced them to economic realities earlier in their teens, insisting that they work to support some of their wants and needs. Their kids saw the great difference between the cost of the things they wanted and their ability to earn the money to buy them.

These parents also prepared their children for the reality of adulthood by insisting that if they didn't go for further education beyond high school, they would be expected to leave home and support themselves. As a result, these children have matured more quickly and taken greater responsibility for their lives.

I think of Brian, basically a good kid, but not a serious student. He definitely didn't want to go to college or vocational school, and his free spirit was unsuited for military service.

As Brian was growing up, his parents believed that if they raised a decent, well-behaved kid, his education would come in time. And it did. Brian moved away from home after high school, according to agreement with his parents. He moved into a large house with several other young men and worked the sales counter at an auto-parts store.

As he watched his peers pursue further education, marry, and begin to show some signs of financial success, he became dissatisfied with his life at age twenty. He asked his parents if he could still take advantage of the four-year option of college. They agreed to let him live at home and go to college, as long as he completed it in four years and moved out when he graduated.

Brian concentrated on business courses, earned a bachelor's degree, and is now managing a large chain retail store. He is married, and he and his wife are saving to buy their own home.

The touching thing about this story is that Brian thanks his parents for letting him struggle after high school. He told them, "If you hadn't insisted I move out after high school, I'd probably still be working that lousy auto parts job and living at home."

Is It Too Late to Start Tough Parenting?

Parents of older teenagers and young adults shouldn't despair if their kids haven't had the benefit of tough parenting all of their lives. It's not too late to start.

Family therapists like to practice early intervention just as medical doctors do. But when we get a late start, we may have to employ strong medicine to turn things around. Take courage. Don't assume your situation is terminal.

Set two goals for yourself: first, refuse to do for your older teenagers what they need to do for themselves; second, be willing to let them take the consequences if they fail to do what they must do to improve their situation. This is how you can do it.

Insist That Your Teenager Be Self-Supporting By insisting that our teenagers become self-supporting, we offer them an education in responsibility. The reason Brian succeeded was that he knew well in advance of high-school graduation that he would have to get out on his own and support himself. Both he and his parents were willing to let him learn the lessons that come through assuming responsibility for your own support.

Mike, though not a typical older teenager, didn't have this advantage. It wasn't until he graduated from high school that his parents realized he needed tough parenting, and they readily admitted that his irresponsible behavior was more a reflection on them than on their son.

At age eighteen, Mike had just graduated from high school, but he didn't know what he wanted to do next. He wasn't a good student, and further education was an unattractive option. He and his parents agreed that he would have the summer to decide about his future. He worked odd jobs to get enough money to finance his leisure time, and though he assured his parents he was working on deciding what to do, he didn't act very concerned about the future.

Labor Day came and went, and still he hadn't decided. His dad, tuning in on Mike's lack of concern about the future, was beginning to get angry. His mom, fearful of a confrontation between Mike and his dad, sought family counseling.

Both Mike and his parents wanted him to be independent, but he maintained that he couldn't afford a place of his own. I suggested that we formulate an action plan to make this possible.

Mike would get a full-time job within a week. He would be expected to work at least forty hours a week, at minimum wage if that was all he could get. The local fast-food places were hiring, so I knew this was possible. He would be permitted to live at home as long as he was turning over $100 a week to his parents to be put in savings for him.

In twelve weeks he would save $1,200. At that time he would be expected to move out on his own. I knew a widow who was willing to rent a room for $65 a week with kitchen privileges. Her house was on a bus line, so even if Mike had to give up his car, he still would be able to get to and from work. At the end of twelve weeks, whether or not Mike was ready, he would be moved out.

Mike looked at me incredulously and said, "You mean you expect me to live in a grubby room on a bus line and spend my whole life doing nothing but working and riding the bus?"

"Yes, I guess you could put it that way," I replied.

"No way, man," Mike said angrily.

I could tell that his dad relished what I was saying, but his mom looked alarmed as she cast glances between the two of them.

As a child, Mike had been shortchanged by his parents. He never had experienced the benefits of tough parenting. Now, at age eighteen, he had to hear things he had never heard before, and understandably he didn't like it.

I felt sorry for Mike. And yet I also wanted to help his parents.

I explained to the family that parents who allow their older teenagers to experience economic hardship do them a favor. It motivates them to consider further education.

Mike saw where I was going with this line of thought and blurted out, "All right—I'll go to college or trade school or something!"

I replied, "I'm afraid that would be a waste of money. It would be unwise to go until you're really ready."

By then our time was up, and I made a date to see Mike's parents by themselves the next week. I was afraid that his mom didn't have the courage to follow through on my suggestion that Mike move out. I also feared that his dad would probably do as he always had done—avoid confrontation by retreating into angry silence.

As it turned out, Mike's dad was ready to go with the plan, but it took three months for Mike's mom to agree to it. Her major problem was a long list of what ifs: what if, after twelve weeks, Mike wasn't working full time; what if he wasn't turning over $100 a week; what if he wouldn't leave on moving day.

I told her, "On moving day, you put all of his things out on the porch and cover them with a tarp."

In disbelief she said, "I can't kick my own son out of the house."

I could understand her reaction. This is why I said at the outset that when we get a late start on tough parenting, we sometimes must take extreme measures.

The story has a happy ending. Mike's parents agreed they would do it. Mike didn't save $100 a week and ignored the widow's offer of a room. On the prearranged moving day, his parents put his things out on the porch. After three months of bouncing around from friend to friend for food and shelter (and not talking to his parents), Mike saw that he was ill-equipped to take care of himself.

I felt sad that Mike's parents had waited so long to get that message across to him and that we had to take such extreme measures to get results. But I was glad that even though these parents had gotten a late start on tough parenting, they had the courage to do what needed to be done.

Mike is now living at home, working full time, and taking twelve hours a semester at his community college. So far it's working, and I think tough parenting is a big part of the reason. But I also commend Mike for not finding fault with his parents for failing to do a better job when he was younger.

Insist That Your Teenager Get Further Education Many teenagers aren't resistant to further education. Indeed, they're willing to go to college or vocational school as a commuting student. But how much of that is motivated by a desire to continue living at home and how much is due to a true appreciation of education, their performance in school will tell.

When your older teenagers *are willing* to live at home while getting further education, do they understand your rules and agree to abide by them? Are *you* as a parent willing to discuss your expectations with them?

Some parents find it difficult to set conditions and rules for the commuting college student. They feel that teenagers who are approaching adulthood ought to be managing their own lives. And if they were going away to college, their parents wouldn't be there to enforce rules.

First of all, teenagers who live on a college campus have to follow rules. These rules are set forth in every college student handbook and enforced by resident advisers and student deans.

Second, by permitting your teenager to live at home, you not only are providing food, shelter, and other perks that are worth a great deal of money, you also are sacrificing peace and quiet you might have if your teenager were self-supporting or away at school. Your teenager has a responsibility to show appreciation for what you're doing by making family life harmonious and by sharing responsibility.

Commuting students must know that we have rules governing both their student status and their living at home. These ought to be discussed *before* matriculation.

1. *Rules governing student status.* When we determine how many credit hours our students will be taking, we can establish how many hours they'll work to pay for their part of their education. College should be a *cooperative* effort between parent and teenager. Students should work as hard as their parents do to get the education. This means students work hard at their studies as well as at a paying job.

Our teenagers need to know that they'll have no more leisure time than we do. Five days a week will be spent going to school, studying, and working a job. Summers should be spent in full-time employment. The money from summer employment should be put aside for school and for necessities such as clothes. Our teenagers become much more conscious of the cost and care of their clothes when they have to buy them.

Sometimes students aren't prepared for the grind of college and working, and they will drop courses and work fewer hours to take the pressure off. If you see this happening, talk to them about it. If we've been realistic about the credit hours and job hours, our students shouldn't have to drop courses because of overload. Most schools have a recommended credit hour/work hour ratio. However, if they're feeling so overwhelmed that they need to readjust their school or work schedule, then by all means negotiate something more workable for both student and parent. But if courses are dropped because of disinterest, then you should be ready to insist that your teenager work more hours. Also, if they have a sizable amount of their own money tied up in tuition, fees, and books, they'll be reluctant to drop courses and lose that money.

Completing college at this rate will take longer than four years, but some students do better by taking a slower pace. This doesn't mean, however, that you have to allow your teenager more than four years at home.

Tough parenting permits our kids (within limits) to operate on their own timetable and permits us freedom to live our lives without having to mesh our plans with theirs. Our youngest son, Jon, took four years to finish two years of college. Fay and I were ready to move when we fulfilled our four-year agreement with Jon. We sold our house and moved away. Our decision created some tense moments with him. But to his credit, he found a place of his own, got a full-time job, got married a couple of years later, and now he and his wife are saving to buy a house. Our relationship to him is stronger now than ever, and a large part of that is based on the respect his mother and I have for what he has accomplished. Tough parenting *does* pay off.

2. *Rules governing family status.* The commuting student still is a member of the family and must assume responsibilities and privileges that go with that status. Sometimes

the commuting student will say, "Look, I'm no longer a kid, and I should be able to come and go as I please."

The answer to that is, "We aren't kids either, but we don't have freedom to come and go as we please. As long as members of the family live together, we all have a responsibility to be accountable and cooperative in order to make life pleasant for everybody."

Our teenagers couldn't have the best of both lives when they were in high school, and they can't now. They can't have all the privileges of family life and none of the responsibilities. A major privilege our teenagers have is free food and shelter. And the only reason they have it is they are a member of the family. No one could pay me enough money to do for a stranger what I lovingly and freely do for my children. If you feel that way, your kids need to know.

Here are some house rules that we should expect our commuting students to observe.

Rule one: We ask them to come and go in a manner and during hours that respect the needs of the others in the family. For example, if they will come in after everyone else has gone to bed, they ought to tell us ahead of time so we won't wonder where they are. Also, when they do come in, they ought to do so without disturbing the rest of the household.

If they're not coming home, they should let us know where they will be and how they can be reached. If they choose not to say so, don't press the matter. But it does bring up another rule.

Rule two: They are accountable. When families live together, *they are accountable to each other.* Accountability offers comfort and security that is essential to the close quarters and emotional vulnerability of family life.

Though older teenagers should be living their own lives guided by moral convictions that are theirs, living at home as a member of the family requires them to modify their behavior while at home out of regard for the others in the family.

Rule three: They must be responsible to pick up after themselves and do household chores. By picking up I mean not leaving books and clothes strewn around the house, not leaving dirty dishes in the family room or kitchen sink. Parents should be sure, however, that they set a positive model by picking up after themselves. Whenever people live together, they have a responsibility to keep the shared living space livable for everyone.

If this rule isn't observed, we may have to do what we did when our kids were in high school. After fair warning, put their things in a bag and out of sight. When they want to know where their things are, charge them a redemption fee of a dollar or more to retrieve them. If they complain that they don't have the money, don't yield. They may get angry and insist that they need the books for school or the shoes for a track meet. But hang tough.

It's far better for our teenagers to be angry at us than for us to be continually angry at them for not keeping the shared living space picked up. Many parents are perpetually angry at their teenagers for not following house rules, but *they* are to blame for not enforcing the rules. Our teenagers need to remember that house rules are part of the price for free room and board.

Rule four: They must take care of their own room and laundry. I suggest that we let commuting students keep their room as they wish, as long as they go through it once a week and collect and wash all the dirty dishes, glasses, and laundry.

Some mothers tell me they would rather do their teenagers' laundry than have them waste extra hot water and soap with a small load of their own. But the little extra we pay in soap and hot water is more than made up by our teenagers learning responsibility for their own clothes.

If they don't have any clean clothes, *don't do their laundry for them.* And if any of their clothes need ironing, teach them how to iron and expect them to do it themselves. And don't be sexist about it. A boy's hand fits an iron as well as a girl's hand does.

Rule five: They are responsible for meals. If our commuting teenagers are going to eat with the family, then family meals have to be arranged with this in mind. If they don't show up for family meals when they say they'll be there, then insist they fend for themselves. They'll have to eat leftovers, if there are any, or make do with whatever's available.

Rule six: They are responsible for their transportation. Commuting students need transportation. If they have a car of their own, they already know that they are responsible for gas, tags, insurance, and upkeep.

If they use the family car, set some guidelines for its use. Should your teenager be allowed to use the car for school and/or social events? What is the teenager's responsibility for gas, insurance, and other expenses? Do you charge twenty-five cents a mile to use the car? If you let your kids charge gas to a credit card, be sure they see the bill and pay their portion of it promptly. Parents should see this as an opportunity to teach teenagers what it costs to run a car.

Parents who complain that their kids don't pay back what they borrow need to face their own failure to hold their kids to agreements. Don't enter into financial agreements if you're not ready to enforce them.

Tough parenting means that we expect them to honor their financial agreements as faithfully as if they had been made with a bank. We should remember that we're already giving them a break on the car by offering something they couldn't possibly get from a bank because they are a financial risk. We also can give them a break by not charging as much for car use as the going commercial rate. We have a marvelous opportunity in agreements like this to teach our older teenagers financial reality and responsibility.

Choosing a School

Schools that offer education beyond high school include community colleges, four-year colleges and universities, and vocational schools.

Community College The community-college program is uniquely American and has much to offer students. Many community colleges offer quality education and have arrangements for the transfer of credits if the student later enrolls in a state four-year college. Check the college catalog to make sure you understand the requirements for transfer of credit if your teenager chooses to go this route. Don't let them enroll under a false assumption and find out later that they can't transfer their credits to a four-year college.

One advantage of attending a community college before going to a four-year school is that the cost is much less than the four-year college. When you take into account the advantage of living at home, a community-college education is quite affordable if parents and teenagers work together.

Another advantage of a community college is cultural continuity. The environment in which students study, live, and work is somewhat similar to high school. The pressure of college study and work may be all some students can handle at one time.

College The purpose of a four-year, liberal-arts college is to develop a person's God-given intellect and expose a person to a wide variety of disciplines: history, science, math, arts, language studies, as well as some fields they may not have explored on a high-school level—sociology, psychology, anthropology, economics, political science, engineering, theology, journalism, environmental studies, or education, to name a few. A liberal-arts degree will not necessarily prepare a person for a specific job, but it helps a person explore the various fields of study he or she may wish to pursue.

The first two years of college usually give a broad exposure to a variety of interests in both the arts and sciences. Extracurricular activities also keep the students in touch with their talents and interests. They'll find their interest develop in a particular direction as time goes by.

1. Non-Christian colleges. The least expensive way to get a college education is through the community- and state-college system in your state of residence. If you and your teenager are able to afford an out-of-state college, either private or state-run, this is an option to consider. Living away from home can be a rich educational experience in itself. Just make sure that your teenagers are carrying a significant part of the financial load. Students who help pay for their education tend to take it seriously.

Some parents are quite dogmatic about not sending their teenager to a non-Christian college. This is often based on the myth that unbelievers are blind to truth and therefore are unsuited to teach Christians anything. The passage often used to support this point of view is 1 Corinthians 2:14–15.

There is a big difference between being blind to truth and being blind to The Truth. A careful examination of the passage reveals that the unbeliever (the "natural man") can't understand *the things of the Spirit of God.* But unregenerate people are still able to perform moral acts. They're able to understand external things. What they're unable to understand is revealed truth, The Truth, things relating to salvation. So it's still possible for your teenagers to receive an excellent education from a non-Christian college, especially if they supplement their academic work with involvement in a local church or in campus groups like InterVarsity Christian Fellowship or Campus Crusade for Christ.

2. *Christian colleges.* Many fine Christian colleges throughout the country integrate Christianity with a liberal-arts education. But be sure they offer educational excellence. The best Christian colleges integrate the things of the Spirit of God with external knowledge ("faith and learning," as many of them say), and do so with high-quality faculty and up-to-date facilities. *Campus Life* magazine publishes a yearly guide to Christian colleges, listing the size, costs, location, and affiliation of most Christian colleges, along with a list of the majors offered at each school.

Vocational School Vocational schools are designed to equip young people with specific skills—like operating office machines or computers—or trade work such as bricklaying or auto mechanics. Check out the vocational school your teenager is considering. Don't be afraid to ask questions.

For example, ask your Better Business Bureau if they have had any complaints about the school. What do the professionals in your community think about the quality of worker the school turns out? The school should be able to refer you to companies who are using their graduates. What are the credentials of the school's faculty? Are they up-to-date on the skills they're teaching? Is the equipment they teach on modern and in good repair? Are the skills learned marketable? For example, if the building industry is in a slump and bricklayers are out of work, your teenager may not want to pursue that trade.

Check the Yellow Pages for companies that may deal with the vocational skill your teenager is interested in. Call the company and ask about the demand for the skill. Skilled workers want the public to have a correct view of their vocation and generally are very helpful in either answering your questions or referring you to someone who can.

Summary

I live on the Chesapeake Bay, where the osprey, a fish hawk, builds its nest on the channel markers outside my window. The osprey's young grow to adult size while they are still in the nest and can be quite demanding about being fed.

I have noticed that at a certain time, the mother and father osprey spend less and less time in the nest, much to their big babies' displeasure. The juvenile osprey may screech all day to be fed, but their cries go unheeded. Every so often they'll face the wind, raise their wings, and become airborne over the nest, just briefly. I get the sense that they're saying, "This is what we do; this must be how we get out of this place."

Then one day, tired of waiting for a free meal, the juvenile osprey become airborne again. But this time they begin to flap their wings and head for the shore, as they have seen their parents do so many times. They find a roost in a tree and for the first time stalk and catch their own fish. They don't do it very well at first.

One day I was working in my yard when I heard a terrific splash in the water not far away. A juvenile osprey had plunged into the water for a fish. A mature bird is strong enough to fly out of the water, shake itself dry in flight, and dine on the fish leisurely in some quiet spot. This juvenile wasn't strong enough to get up out of the water with its fish. After several unsuccessful tries, it started to swim to the shore with its wings, like a swimmer doing the butterfly stroke. When the young osprey got to shore, I could see that it still had the fish. I could almost hear it say to the fish, "After all this, there's no chance you're getting away."

With fish firmly locked in its talons, the osprey hopped up on the shore and voraciously tore the fish apart, consuming it in a short time. Then, after preening and drying itself in the sun, the osprey took off to another tree to do it again.

As I watched the osprey, I thought, *Hunger does a great deal to teach young ospreys to fly and catch their own fish. God help us to be parents as tough as the mother and father osprey.*

12

When Things Get Out of Hand

If you've been working at tough parenting, you probably won't face the problems I discuss in this chapter. But if you do, don't despair and feel that you can do nothing. We don't give up on tough parenting, even though our children may be in their teens or older. Sometimes both we and our kids need the perspective of adulthood to see what went wrong, and talking together as a family, we can understand what happened and do something about it.

But this means that both parents and children must avoid blaming. It's not helpful to deny responsibility and put it on parent or child. Healing of wounds requires that both parents and kids be honest with themselves and each other about their failings.

When we look at family problems, the cause usually isn't the parent *or* the child. It's usually the *chemistry* of the relationship. Vinegar and baking soda look quite stable by themselves, but if we put them together, we have a foaming mess.

I don't mean that each is equally responsible for the

problem. That may be. But parents unnecessarily tough on very compliant children or children who are determined to rebel no matter what their parents do must be especially careful not to justify their behavior if the family is to experience healing.

For example, the father who says, "You made me treat you harshly with spankings and restrictions because you were such a difficult child" may need to look at his own insecurities as a parent and understand that he behaved harshly not because the child needed it but because he was afraid he would lose control. Likewise, children who blame their parents for harsh treatment may need to look at their own behavior as children. They often feel they didn't deserve the discipline they received because they don't know how difficult they were.

When things get out of hand, this kind of soul searching, confession, and reconciliation is needed more than ever. But it's essential that *both* the parents and kids are willing to understand the part they played in the disintegration of the relationship and that *both* are willing to do what is necessary to save it. Just as one person can't save a marriage in which a spouse is determined to continue destructive behavior, one member of the family can't save it when the others are unwilling to do their part.

You may say, "That's all well and good. But what do we do when we have a son who reaches a state of rebellion that's beyond our control? What do we do with a daughter who, in spite of our best attempts at sex education and guidance, becomes pregnant? What do we do about a son who is chronically depressed and talks about suicide? What do we do about the son or daughter who was never a serious problem to us but announces that he or she is homosexual and intends to pursue a homosexual lifestyle?" Tough parenting still is necessary.

Kids Out of Control

Jean's fifteen-year-old son, Trent, was out of control. He would skip school, go out at night whenever he pleased, and return home sometimes as late as one or two o'clock in the morning. When she tried to talk to him about it, he verbally abused her and let her know that he was going to do whatever he pleased. Sometimes he got physical with her and pushed her around when she didn't do what he wanted.

Trent's father was utterly indifferent to what was going on and lost himself in his work and activities. He stayed away from home as much as possible. As far as he was concerned, the boy didn't exist.

I felt that Trent was going to get his father to acknowledge his existence, even if he had to murder someone to do it. And I told his mother so.

"What can I do?" she asked helplessly. "His father won't help, and Trent is too big for me to handle."

"When Trent goes on a tirade and starts abusing you verbally, walk away from him," I told her.

"But he follows me around and keeps at me until he gets his way."

"In that case, get a magazine, lock yourself in the bathroom, and read until Trent goes away."

"But he'll break down the door and probably hurt me."

"In that case, call the police."

"I couldn't do that."

"Why?"

"They'd probably take him away."

"Not unless you signed a complaint against him and were willing to go to court. Are you willing to do that?"

"No."

"Neither I nor the police can help you if you're not willing to get tough with Trent. I guess things will have to get a lot worse before something is done about Trent. Maybe he'll have to commit a crime before someone takes action."

Parents' unwillingness to get tough with their kids is a major problem that keeps counselors and juvenile authorities from intervening. Police are reluctant to do anything about domestic disputes because parents rarely file complaints and take the matter to court.

I'm heartened to hear about cities that are strengthening their laws to bring kids under control. These cities are beginning to make parents responsible. Not long ago the town of Dermott, Arkansas, imposed an eleven o'clock curfew and made parents accountable for crimes committed by their children. Since then, juvenile crime has fallen fifty percent. Parents can be charged with misdemeanors if they don't try to keep their children under age eighteen at home after curfew. They can be charged if they fail to keep weapons out of the hands of children under age thirteen or if they allow their children to possess controlled substances in their home.

Charles Gibson, city attorney, says that no parent suffers because of an incorrigible kid. They just have to show they're doing all they can. No parent is punished for a first offense. They receive a letter of warning. But a second offense is punishable by twenty hours of community service, a $500 fine, and/or thirty days in jail. The law works, and not because their jail is filled with parents. Since the law went into effect, no parent has been jailed, and only three have received warnings. Yet, crime is way down. Clearly, parents are taking greater responsibility.[1]

Laws are on the books to help parents. But they have to be willing to get tough. Sometimes our kids will respond just *knowing* that we are willing to go to court if necessary.

One father reports that when his thirteen-year-old son violated restrictions and no longer responded to spankings, this is exactly what he did. He said, "One evening after supper, which Kevin made unpleasant for the whole family, I told him to get in the car. Why he decided to comply, I don't know, except that I may have looked more determined than ever to intervene, and he may have been curious.

"It was dark as we drove to the county juvenile detention facility. It was surrounded by a high barbed-wire fence. The floodlights and fog contributed to the somber mood.

"'Do you know what this place is?' I asked.

"'No.'

"'It's the county juvenile detention facility.'

"Kevin looked at me wide-eyed, as if to say, 'What are you trying to tell me?'

"I said, 'Kevin, I'm going to tell you this just once. You either do what your mother and I ask you to do, or you can live here with their rules.'

"Kevin knew that I never bluff. In all of his thirteen years, I never said I would do anything in the way of discipline that I failed to do.

"After a few minutes of silence, tears started down Kevin's cheeks. 'Dad,' he said, 'I promise I'll do what you and Mom tell me to do. Just don't put me in this place!'

"I leaned over, hugged him, and said, 'That's all we want, Kevin. We love you, but we can't make family life work without your cooperation.'

"Though Kevin gave us static throughout his teen years, we never had to go through this again. He turned out to be a fine young man who went to college, married, and now has children of his own."

Young and Pregnant

Sexual activity of teenagers between ages fifteen and nineteen has increased over the past fifteen years from thirty to fifty percent—about 5 million girls and 6.5 million boys. In 1950, half of the teenage mothers were married when they first gave birth. By 1980, only thirty percent were married.[2] What are parents supposed to do when they find that their teenage daughter is pregnant?

Thirty years ago, a lot of pressure was put on the girl to marry the child's father. But teenage marriages don't work well. Pregnancy isn't a good reason to marry.

Parents who are pro-choice may be tempted to encourage an abortion, particularly if their daughter also is pro-choice. But they need to stop and seriously consider the emotional impact that abortion may have on their daughter. It's dangerous to generalize and cite studies that prove or disprove the emotional impact of abortion on a mother. Your daughter is an individual with her own feelings and emerging values. Quite apart from the studies, how does *she* feel about aborting her child? I find that girls can be pro-choice when talking about someone else's baby but have different feelings about their own unborn baby.

The pro-life parent should encourage the teenager to bring the child to term and put it up for adoption. Not only does this choice preserve life, it gives the baby a chance for a good life with loving parents. It also encourages teenagers to see that actions have consequences and that they need to take responsibility both for their actions and their consequences.

When Your Daughter Wants an Abortion A larger problem emerges when a girl *insists* she is going to get an abortion and her parents believe abortion is murder. What then?

When our kids become teenagers, they take life-and-death issues into their own hands in many different ways. It may be pregnancy or suicide.

Parents aren't always able to influence the decisions their teenagers make. Sometimes we must let go and let those life-and-death decisions be theirs along with the consequences.

Teenagers who are determined to abort are much like teenagers who are determined to commit suicide. If they're determined, they'll do it. And sometimes when they see that we accept our powerlessness to do anything about their life-and-death decision, they'll reconsider.

My concern for the teenager who is determined to have an abortion against her parents' wishes is that she may seek an abortion under conditions that endanger her life. While on one hand, pro-life parents can't bring themselves to arrange an abortion, they may find that the best of all the bad alternatives is to stand aside and let their daughter take responsibility for her decision to abort and for making the necessary arrangements. If she does go that route, she needs to know that even though your convictions don't allow you to have anything to do with the abortion, you still love her. The prodigal can come home.

When Your Daughter Wants to Keep the Baby Another dilemma that parents of a pregnant teenager face is what to do when their daughter wants to keep the baby. Teenage girls sometimes think childbirth will give them a sense of worth, identity, and someone to love and love them. Utterly unprepared for the demands of mothering, teenage mothers find that the novelty quickly wears off, and they begin to resent the demands the child makes on them, particularly when their friends want them to socialize. When the teenage mother is living with her parents, she tends to push more and more of the responsibility of childcare on them. Here's where parents need to be tough. It's a constant battle to make the teenage mother do all that needs to be done, and the list is formidable: feeding, bathing, dressing, diapering, walking, playing, getting up at night, laundry, toilet training, and taking the child to the pediatrician.

As long as your daughter is willing to carry the primary care of the child and go to school and work, you may have little choice. But if your daughter pushes the child on you because it's interfering with her social life, you may have to do the tough thing and let her know that she'll have to support herself.

It's not easy for a grandparent to see a grandchild live in squalor with an irresponsible teenage mother. One angry parent told me, "My daughter has a kid, and now it's my responsibility to raise him. I put my daughter out, but I can't let her have this child. That would be criminal neglect."

The parent was in a serious bind. She knew that she couldn't handle the child herself. And I was afraid that if she sought custody of the child, she would be an angry grandparent. She might unintentionally take her anger out on the child. Here again we had to choose the best of unhappy alternatives.

I encouraged the parent to turn the child over to her daughter with a warning: Take care of the child or answer to the county social-services division on a complaint of parental neglect. The parent hung tough and did it. The daughter now is awaiting a court date to face neglect charges, and her child has been taken from her by the state.

I don't know the quality of foster care the child will get, but I have a hunch that it will be better than she would get from an angry, ailing grandmother or a neglectful mother. My wife and I were the foster parents of two girls, and I think we did a pretty good job.

What Do You Say to Your Son? When your son is the father of the child, what do you say to him?

You will need to help your son face the consequences of his actions and take responsibility for the pregnancy. He can take responsibility by offering support to his girlfriend in two ways: emotionally and financially.

Sometimes, however, the parents of the girl block the boy from offering any kind of support. This only cuts the unwed father off from dealing with his own feelings of guilt and responsibility. If this happens, you should try to arrange a conference with your son and the girl's parents to find out what *they* expect of your son. Help your son deal calmly with any unreasonable demands, and try to come to a consensus on how your son can help. If they still want nothing to do with your son, at least by talking with them he is dealing with the issue of his responsibility and, if nothing else, can feel that he tried.

Depression and Suicide

Depression in children usually shows itself in a number of symptoms. They feel sad, worthless, tend to be aggressive, have difficulty with sleep, poor school performance, lack of social interest, physical complaints, and a change in appetite. But not all depressed children are suicide risks.

Nancy Grannan, age nineteen, was one of six young people who committed suicide by carbon monoxide poisoning within days of one another in the spring of 1987. Nancy was depressed over her failed marriage. But was that enough to make her kill herself?

She left behind a piece of paper with the lyrics to "Fade to Black," a song sung by her favorite heavy-metal rock group, Metallica. The song was an unabashed suicide invitation, which expressed Nancy's suicidal feelings. She had felt *hopeless*.

The Three Hs Depressed people who feel hopeless are suicide risks. But they show an observable progression from depression to hopelessness. This progression some-times is called the three Hs: hapless, helpless, and hope-less.

1. *Hapless.* People who feel hapless experience a series of bad breaks or misfortunes. Whether or not they really had any control over the events is irrelevant, because they *feel* hapless. Often this feeling rises out of our teenagers' failure to grow up emotionally and take responsibility for doing something about the misfortunes that befall them. Hapless teenagers often are people who never developed coping skills and never had to; someone else always took care of things, usually their parents.

Hapless teenagers often are blamers. Rather than see the part they play in their own misfortunes, either by failing to avoid them or failing to overcome them, they blame others. In doing so, they excuse themselves from the blame for their troubles or the need to clean up the mess their lives are in.

2. *Helpless.* Hapless people quickly become helpless. To hear them tell it, not only are they the victims of misfortunes beyond their control, but now—wallowing in the misery of their misfortune—they declare that they can do nothing about it.

Helplessness often becomes a form of adjustment for manipulative people who have family and friends used to helping helpless souls. These are people who are afraid of the consequences of not helping. They're afraid that the helpless teenager may sink deeper into depression, so they reach down and pull him or her out of trouble once again.

This doesn't mean we let our teenagers suffer the pain of misfortune to the point where they're ready to kill them-selves. If teenagers talk about committing suicide, we should take them seriously and hospitalize them for observation to determine if they really want to take their lives.

Not all teenagers who die by their own hand intend to kill themselves. Many teenagers use suicidal behavior as a way to manipulate. They hope that a non-lethal suicide attempt will get them what they want, but the attempt turns out to be more lethal than they intended. Or they may make a lethal attempt, like a drug overdose, expecting to be discovered. But they die when their lethal attempt isn't discovered.

Whether a teenager really wants to die or if the behavior is manipulative, hospitalization is necessary. If the teenager is serious, intervention is needed. If it's a manipulation, hospitalization usually stops suicide games.

Teenagers who never have to solve their own problems and are always bailed out by well-meaning parents and friends tend to become manipulators. But it cripples them, making them incapable of helping themselves, simply because they never had to try. This sets the stage for hopelessness.

3. *Hopeless.* When young people who have never developed coping skills experience defeat after defeat, life becomes such an intolerable burden that they become preoccupied with escaping from it. Some escape a little at a time, through drugs and alcohol. They develop an addiction and kill themselves by overdose or carelessness.

Parents should realize that when I talk about trials being important to the development of coping skills, I'm assuming that our teenagers are being shown what their alternatives are and that stress isn't overwhelming. Teenagers need to see that they have options, and they need protection against overwhelming stress.

When stress is overwhelming, they experience what is called *decompensation*. This occurs when the person's usual coping mechanisms fail to relieve the stress and the ability to think and act is impaired by physical and emotional exhaustion. Sometimes it goes as far as a break with reality. Other times the reaction is more a sense of confusion and an inability to think clearly.

Many teenagers who have attempted suicide tell of thoughts and feelings that are descriptive of decompensation. When the stress has been occurring over a long period and the person is decompensating, he or she is likely at that moment to feel utterly hopeless and attempt suicide, particularly if the means are readily available.

Most people who resort to suicide aren't crazy. They are desperate people, sometimes only dimly aware of what they're doing. Hospitalization is necessary to protect them from themselves and to help them deal with their sense of hopelessness.

When Your Teenager Talks of Suicide What do you say to teenagers who talk about committing suicide? We must realize that we can't prevent them from committing suicide if they're really determined to do it. They'll find the means and the occasion.

If your teenager has been diagnosed as a suicide risk, and after hospitalization and treatment he or she is still determined, you may want to consider long-term hospitalization for your child's protection.

Sometimes teenagers won't threaten to commit suicide or act sufficiently suicidal to warrant hospitalization. But they'll talk about suicide to alarm and manipulate their parents. It often is helpful for the teenager to hear the parent say, "I love you very much, and I would be deeply grieved if you should kill yourself. But I realize that if you're really determined to do it, there's nothing I can do to stop you."

Even parents who have done everything to prevent teen suicide must come to the place where they accept their teenagers' destructive decisions. The entire responsibility for our children turning out right can't rest on us. Our children also bear responsibility. If we don't accept this, we'll be ever-grieving parents, wondering what we could have done differently.

Homosexuality

Homosexuality has a way of tearing at the emotions of families like no other problem they face, particularly when parent-child relations have been cordial and the parents adore their child. But it's not difficult only for parents. It's difficult for teenagers to acknowledge that they wrestle with homosexual urges. How can they disappoint parents who feel that they've done a good job? It's difficult for them to say, "Mom, Dad, I appreciate all you've done to bring me to adulthood, but something went wrong. I find my own sex more attractive than the opposite sex."

Don't Be Quick to Label I once had a client say to me, "People aren't homosexuals until they decide to be." This was a man who was wrestling with homosexual urges but refused to call himself a homosexual. It was a thought-provoking statement, and I asked him to elaborate.

"I've wrestled all my life with homosexual urges," he told me. "In the flesh, I desire men more than women. But I realized a long time ago that my attitude has a lot to do with the problem. I can choose to surrender, label myself as a homosexual, and become part of the homosexual community. Or I can refuse the label and accept these unwanted urges as a burden I have to bear, just as the alcoholic who wants a drink or the heterosexual who is in a sexually unfulfilling marriage."

This encounter made me realize the importance of properly handling young people with homosexual urges. We must help them understand that they don't *have* to accept the homosexual label just because they have same-sex attraction. As long as they're unwilling to accept homosexual behavior, there's hope. This doesn't mean they won't slip. It means that the *commitment not to give in to the unhealthy behavior* is all-important, just as it is with the recovering alcoholic.

When Your Teenager Doesn't Want Help Teenagers who accept the label, identify with the homosexual community, and don't want help present a special problem to parents. The problem is further magnified when the teenagers live at home, want all the benefits of family life, but are unwilling to commit to change.

Teenagers need to understand that parents often feel that they are *subsidizing* a homosexual lifestyle when they support teenagers who are unwilling to get help. If homosexually active teenagers are going to live at home, they must be willing to give up that activity and get help to stay straight.

Tough parenting recognizes that family life doesn't work as long as teenagers are unwilling to do something about their behavior. Family life is a matter of cooperation and compromise. Parents would expect this of an alcoholic teenager; they should expect it of the teenager caught in homosexuality.

Help for Homosexuals Teenagers wrestling with homosexuality must understand that they're not expected suddenly to feel attraction to the opposite sex. The way out is gradual. Intensive professional counseling with a Christian therapist and involvement in a support group will be of great help if they are committed to the process and willing to remain celibate for as long as is necessary. Consult the Appendix for a reading list and for information about support groups.

Professional Help When Things Get Out of Hand

Christian families sometimes resist getting professional help when things get out of hand because of their view of psychology and the Bible. They believe that the answers to all their problems are in the Bible, and that's all the help they need.

All of the Bible is true. It was given to teach us things that we couldn't learn from observing nature. But all truth is not in the Bible. We get truth from special revelation (the Bible) and natural revelation (nature). Both are important.

If things have gotten out of hand in your family, find someone who has had training in both theology and psychology to help you understand what's going on. You may be committed to living a life that pleases God, but you may be unaware that you're keeping it from happening because you don't see how your personality is affecting relationships.

One regret I have as a father is that I didn't understand that a lot of conflict I had with my oldest son was the result of my own insecurity as a young parent. I was afraid that I would lose control, and as a consequence, I tended to be harder on him than I think was necessary. I still would have employed the tough parenting approach, but there's a difference between being tough and being rigid. The tough parent is able to entertain several options; the rigid parent must have it *his* way.

The beautiful thing about our relationship now is that we're able to go back, look at what happened, and correct those mistakes. A dynamic family is always growing. We must not suppose that if we didn't do it right from the very beginning, all is lost. Indeed, the vista of adulthood offers both parents and children a marvelous vantage point from which we can see what went wrong, resolve it together, and then move on to reach new heights in our growth as a family.

13

You Can Do It

Young parents often voice fears about raising children in today's world—it's a dangerous place. Yes, the world can seem to be full of evil influences and dangers. But it's also an exciting place, full of beauty, full of opportunity for involvement in God's world. As Christians we can have the confidence that God is in control, that the whole world is under his dominion.

I think of several large families I know, families each with five or six children. Did they hesitate to have children? Did they feel it was too much of a risk to bring children into a dangerous world?

Quite the opposite. One couple expressed their perspective eloquently. "When we see the evil in the world, when we see the dangers our children will face, we are all the more convinced that the world needs more children who have experienced the love of God in a warm, accepting, disciplining family. These children can model that love, acceptance, and forgiveness in all their relationships; they can reflect God's character in dynamic ways. Rather than being afraid of what our children will face, we are more strongly determined to be godly parents, to influence our world through our children, preparing them to cope with danger and difficulty, preparing them to be leaders, preparing them to be effective parents."

Doing Something for a Dangerous World

Christians are called the salt of the earth. Just as salt prevents food from spoiling, our role is to prevent rot in society. Christian children who learn through tough parenting that love and firmness go together help to make our world a better place to live.

Why is it, then, that so many young couples are hesitant or uncertain about parenting? In the 1960s, having children began to lose its appeal for many couples, particularly for mothers. Opportunities for women flourished, and as they saw attractive career options that promised intellectual stimulation and fulfillment, they entered the work world at a rate unparalleled in American history. These women valued children, but they also wanted careers.

Now, thirty years later, couples are beginning to have second thoughts. Many women have found that a career outside the home isn't nearly as rewarding as they supposed it would be. The idea of returning to homemaking and mothering as a full-time job has increasing appeal. Other women, because of economic necessity or a fulfilling career, continue to work outside of the home, but are finding a new enthusiasm for parenting. One career mom told me, "I must have been naïve to think that being an account executive with a large advertising firm would bring more meaning to my life. After twenty-five years of being a mom and career woman, I'll tell you that I've gotten a lot more fulfillment as a parent than in my career with all of its perks, a good salary, and respectability as a professional. My son is an elementary-school principal.

When I see him deal lovingly but firmly with his kids, I say to myself, 'Lady, you may be Ms. Advertising to your peers, but this is what really counts.'"

Setting Parental Fears to Rest

Even though parenting is again becoming a meaningful occupation, couples today still express fear. As I look back at our decision to become parents forty years ago, I realize that today's couples have fears that Fay and I didn't have.

We still laugh about my first experience with a baby— our son Steve. I never even had held a baby, and suddenly I was the father of a squirming, gurgling, eight-pound baby boy. I asked Fay, "How do you go about picking up a baby?" My mind went back to my childhood when I built balsa-wood-and-tissue-paper model airplanes that had to be handled very carefully.

Fay laughed. "You won't hurt him. The main thing is to support his head." She showed me how, and then I tried.

As a young father of twenty-two, I held my first baby, but it wasn't long before I was helping with the feeding, bathing, diapering, and comforting of this new little person. I often asked myself whatever made me think that I could do the job of fathering when I had absolutely no training or experience. And then I think of couples today who are afraid to take on the job. What has changed?

The Technocratic Mind-Set

We live in a highly technical society, built and managed by people who have spent years in formal education and training. We tend to think that no job can be done well without intensive training.

Given this mind-set and the plethora of books, articles, and television programs about parenting, would-be parents understandably feel overwhelmed by the task. But all the books in the world can't teach a parent to provide the two most important ingredients to successful parenting—love and acceptance.

These things can't be taught. They're caught by exposure to healthy families and are passed from generation to generation by contagious parents who feel love and acceptance.

In a healthy climate like this, we are able to learn the skills of parenting and be successful at it. I may have all the possible book knowledge about parenting, but if I don't help my child feel loved and accepted, I'm nothing.

Perhaps someone will say, "I came from a dysfunctional family and never learned to get and give love in a healthy way. Is there hope for me?"

Yes. We can learn as adults how to receive and give love. One of my most rewarding experiences in life was working with a young man named Rick, who wanted to marry and have a family but felt that he didn't know how to love.

Rick grew up in a home with a very dominant mother and passive father. He never saw a caring relationship between them so he had no idea what a loving relationship between a husband and wife was. And his relationship with his mother made matters worse. Rick's mother tried to control him by doing things for him. When he resisted by doing everything he possibly could do for himself, she berated him for not appreciating her. He grew up feeling that being loved by someone meant being controlled by that person.

He met a wonderful young woman, Tara, who loved him deeply. And yet he was afraid of her love and found it difficult to show love in return. But after they dated for a couple of years, Tara and I began to notice a change in Rick. She told me that he was more willing to let her do things for him, and he reciprocated her kindness by thanking her, and even kissing her on the cheek—a display of affection he had never shown before.

When I asked Rick if he had seen any change in himself, he said yes. I asked him what had happened. He told me, "For the past couple of years I've been spending a lot of time with Tara's family. At first I was amazed at how thoughtful they were of each other's feelings and how they showed their affection for each other. They accepted me without question, and they didn't seem suspicious of each other's motives—like, 'Watch out. Someone's going to gain the upper hand.'

"Then I began to notice the same thing when we would visit friends and meet their parents. They respected each other's needs too. I realized that giving and getting love and respecting the needs of others in the family was not only normal, but something I too was beginning to feel for Tara and her family. I no longer was afraid of love."

Rick and Tara are now married, and they're expecting their first child. Though Rick sometimes wonders what kind of father he'll be, Tara tells him, "You'll be a *great* father. You learned to be a wonderful husband, didn't you?" Rick just smiles.

Don't Let the Experts Take Over

The past forty years have witnessed a proliferation of experts. Though many of us have credentials that permit us to speak authoritatively on the subject of parenting, we can speak only of what is *generally* true of children in given circumstances.

Just remember, *you* are the expert on your child. No other person knows your child better than you do. You understand your child's disposition, temperament, and personality. Pray and ask God to show you what tough parenting means for each of your children. Does your child need to experience more of the bumps and bruises of life to learn coping skills? Or does your child need a bit of protecting from overwhelming adversity? In what circumstances will your child strengthen and flourish? Then trust God to guide your instincts.

Our Kids Are Responsible Too

Another difference I see in parenting today is that parents feel completely responsible for how their children turn out. I don't recall feeling this way as a young parent. In the past forty years, psychologists have blamed children's maladjusted behavior on their parents. Now that these children are parents, they don't want to hear that *they* are responsible for botching the job too.

We parents certainly must own up to doing a lot of things wrong. But many times children themselves create situations that have an important bearing on what happened. I think of Richard, an introverted, socially maladjusted twenty-year-old counselee who lashed out at his parents, "You controlled my friendships with an iron fist all of my life, and now you wonder why I can't relate to people."

His mother replied, "You mean you don't know why? Don't you remember that when you started kindergarten, we had to take you out of school because you would fly into a rage and beat up the other kids? We even faced a lawsuit when you clubbed another little boy with a metal truck! You don't remember the years of counseling we went through with you? You seemed to grow out of these fits of rage as the years passed. But we were never sure when someone might cross you, and you would hurt them badly."

Richard was dumbfounded. He hadn't remembered any of this behavior. But his mother's revelation had a profound effect on turning him around. When he realized that he was a large part of the problem, he was able to accept responsibility to get his life in order.

We're Not Alone

Maybe it's the technocratic mind-set or the abundance of experts giving us advice on parenting, but sometimes we forget that we're not alone. God invented parenting, and he intends to make it work. He promises to give us all the help we need.

When we're feeling that too much depends on us, we might remember God's rebuke to Job: "Does the hawk take flight by your wisdom and spread his wings toward the south?" (Job 39:26). We're not expected to do the job of tough parenting by our own wisdom. Adversity, working in tandem with our children's survival instincts, generates growth that the best informed, most energetic parent can't match. It's humbling to realize that it's not by our wisdom the hawk flies south or our children grow up to be well-adjusted, self-supporting adults. Yes, we protect them from overwhelming adversity and we teach them survival skills. But ultimately, only they can master the skills essential for survival.

The Hawk Flies South

The nights are cooler now by the Chesapeake Bay, and the days are shorter. The parent ospreys are gone, and the nest is in tatters from storms and wind. The fledgling roosts in a tall pine by the water, stalking its prey. Occasionally it returns to the empty nest, as if reluctant to give up what it has known as home all of its life. And then it is airborne again, back to the hunt.

It circles, folds its wings, and with talons extended, it hits the water. By now its wings are strong enough to lift its catch out of the water, and none too soon, because it faces a new and unfamiliar task. The ospreys are beginning to migrate to their winter feeding grounds in Brazil's wild upland country. Flying across the Gulf of Mexico and Central America, they will travel 4000 miles!

I think, as I watch, that this fledgling has never migrated before. But God has equipped this young bird with the instinct and strength to do it. Its parents aren't here to pack a lunch. Does it know that migrating ospreys often take a fish along, just in case food isn't available along the way?

I tell myself, "No matter. He's young and strong. If he forgets his lunch, I bet it's the only time he does. Hunger has a way of bringing out the best in the hunter."

Soon he will be gone. I thank him for what he has taught me.

And now the osprey soars,
on wings made strong
by blessed adversity,
a gift from a loving father.

Resources

Chapter 3

Day Care. For more information about finding and evaluating day-care facilities, see chapter 9 of my book *Single Parenting* (Grand Rapids, Michigan: Zondervan, 1992).

Chapter 5

Television. Parents concerned about the impact of television on their children may want to write:

> Christian Leaders for Responsible Television
> P.O. Box 2440
> Tupelo, MS 38803

For a biweekly newsletter about television and kids, write:

> Between the Lines
> 325 Pennsylvania Ave. S.E.
> Washington, DC 20003

Chapter 6

Your Child's Development. Parents interested in books, tapes, and games that address the developmental needs of children may want to write for the catalog "Childswork/Childsplay," a resource that is for the most part helpful.

Center for Applied Psychology
Third Floor
441 N. 5th St.
Philadelphia, PA 19123

Reading to Your Children. This is an excellent way to spend time with them and inspire them to good reading. *Classics to Read Aloud to Your Children* by William F. Russell (New York: Crown Publishers, 1981) offers reading lists for age 5 and up, age 8 and up, and age 11 and up.

Chapter 7

Sexuality. Two good books about masturbation are *The Stork Is Dead* by Charlie Shedd (Waco, Texas: Word, 1976) and *My Beautiful Feeling* by Walter and Ingrid Trobisch (Downers Grove, Illinois: InterVarsity Press, 1976).

Chapter 11

College. You may generate some enthusiasm for college in your high-school seniors by sending them to Hillsdale Hostel, advertised as "a unique learning vacation for seniors." The college also publishes "Imprimis," an excellent newsletter of conservative opinion on social and political issues.

Hillsdale College
Hillsdale, Michigan 49242 1-800-334-8904

Chapter 12

Homosexuality. The organization Regeneration, Inc. publishes a newsletter whose stated purpose is "to bring God's healing to homosexuals and to help the Body of Christ in reaching out to those caught in homosexuality."

Regeneration, Inc. also works with Love and Action, an AIDS outreach based in Annapolis—(301) 268-3442.

>Regeneration
>P.O. Box 9830
>Baltimore, MD 21284-9830
>(301) 661-0284
>TTY/TDD for hearing impaired (301) 882-6312

Exodus International offers information about ex-gay ministries in North America and overseas. They offer literature, support groups, and information to parents.

>Exodus International
>P.O. Box 2121
>San Rafael, CA 94912
>(415) 454-1017

Notes

Introduction

[1]Michael L. Peck, Norman L. Farberow, and Robert E. Litman, *Youth Suicide* (New York: Springer Publishing Company, 1985), 19–20.

Chapter 5

[1]Eleanor Emmons Maccoby and Carol Nagy Jacklin, *The Psychology of Sex Differences* (Stanford: Stanford University Press, 1974), 205.
[2]Ibid., 207
[3]Ibid.
[4]Ibid., 209
[5]Ibid.

Chapter 6

[1]Charles B. Clayman, ed., *The American Medical Association Home Medical Encyclopedia* (New York: Random House, 1989), vol. 1, 269.
[2]Maccoby and Jacklin, *The Psychology of Sex Differences*, 363.
[3]Dr. Fitzhugh Dodson, *How to Father* (New York: The New American Library, Inc., 1975), 108.

Chapter 8

[1]Judith Marks Mishne, *Clinical Work with Adolescents* (New York: The Free Press, 1986), 13.
[2]Ibid.

Chapter 10

[1]Jacqueline Simenauer and David Carroll, *Singles: The New Americans* (New York: New American Library, 1982), 320–21.

Chapter 11

[1]"Singleness In America," Bureau of Census Statistical Brief, SB-4-89, November 1989.

Chapter 12

[1]*USA Today*, Sept. 15, 1982, 10A.
[2]*Parents* (March 1987): 196.